A GARDEN FOR CUTTING

Gardening for Flower Arrangements

MARGARET PARKE

PHOTOGRAPHS BY PETER MARGONELLI

Stewart, Tabori & Chang
New York

Text copyright © 1993 Margaret Parke

Photographs copyright © 1993 Peter Margonelli except for photographs on pages 5, 13, 16 (right), 19, 21 (bottom), 36–37, 40, 41, 43, 44 (top), 45, 46–47, 48, 51, 54 (left), 62, 68, 69 (both), 70 (top), 112, 113, 117 (right), 124–125, 153 (bottom), 168, 169 (right), 171, 172, 178, 182, 183, 185 (left), and 186, all of which are © 1993 Margaret Parke.

The map on pages 222–223 is courtesy of the Agricultural Research Service, USDA.

Published in 1993 by Stewart, Tabori & Chang, Inc.
575 Broadway, New York, New York 10012

Library of Congress Cataloging-in-Publication Data
Parke, Margaret.
    A garden for cutting : gardening for flower arrangements / Margaret Parke ; photographs by Peter Margonelli.
        p.   cm.
    Includes bibliographical references and index.
    ISBN 1-55670-250-7
    1. Flower gardening.   2. Flower arrangement.   3. Cut flowers.
I. Title.
SB405.P22   1993   93-10806
635.9'66—dc20   CIP

Distributed in the U.S. by Workman Publishing,
708 Broadway, New York, New York 10003

Represented in Canada by Canadian Manda Group,
P.O. Box 920, Station U, Toronto, Ontario M8Z 5P9

Distributed in all other territories (except Central and South America) by Melia Publishing Services,
P.O. Box 1639, Maidenhead, Berkshire SL6 6YZ England

Central and South American accounts should contact Export Sales Manager, Stewart, Tabori & Chang.

Printed in Hong Kong

10 9 8 7 6 5 4 3 2

PAGE 1 *Fresh garden flowers and foliage are unsurpassed for creating bouquets that bring joy and beauty indoors, where their details can be appreciated up close. Here blue bellflowers (Campanula sp.) grow up between the ribbed foliage of hostas.*

PAGE 2 *The challenge of mixing and matching plants in pleasing combinations in the garden and in the vase affords great pleasure. Brilliant blue delphiniums and wine-purple hollyhocks stand tall against the hazy pinkish plumes and purple foliage of smokebush.*

PAGE 3 *An armload of gleanings from a summer garden near Portland, Oregon, include rich orange daylilies, blue globes of echinops, yarrow, Queen Anne's lace, spikes of blue Russian sage (Perovskia atriplicifolia), gold wild mullein, gray-leaved artemisia, and a giant leaf of Gunnera manicata.*

PAGE 5 *Lilacs, viburnum, and peonies—cherished flowers of the author's childhood—are still favorites for spring bouquets. At times the "best" cut flowers are not those that last the longest, but the ones that recall happy occasions.*

PAGE 6 TOP—*Caption appears on page 24;* MIDDLE—*Caption appears on page 80;* BOTTOM—*Caption appears on page 114.*

PAGE 7 TOP—*Caption appears on page 138;* MIDDLE—*Caption appears on page 156;* BOTTOM—Digitalis *plant profile appears on page 170.*

To the memory of my mother and father

CONTENTS

PREFACE

To imagine the earth without plants that flower is next to impossible, although at one time the planet was devoid of the color and gaiety that flowers bring, and only the serene greens of ferns, conifers, and cycads covered the land. Without flowering trees and shrubs, the very contours of the earth would be different, and without flowers, their fruits, and their animal pollinators, the sights, scents, and tastes of our world would lack many of the delights we take for granted. ❧ It is just as impossible to imagine a garden without flowers. Whether one gardens mainly to have fresh gourmet vegetables that are free of pesticides or

specializes in raising herbs or dwarf conifers, some portion of the garden is always given over to growing flowers. This testifies over and over again to the power the beauty of flowers wields over us.

Although it isn't necessary to take up flower gardening in order to indulge in beautiful flowers, it helps mightily if one does. Individual temperament will decide whether we will take pleasure in simply looking at flowers in the garden or whether we will bring them indoors to enjoy them in new ways. While flower arranging is not an inevitable pursuit for all flower gardeners, it is a natural, enjoyable, and accessible byway of flower gardening.

This book is for those who want to take full advantage of the garden's potential to provide material for flower arrangements. I hope it will also entice those gardeners who hold that the rightful place for garden flowers is in the garden, thus limiting the wider joys that flowers can bring to daily living.

The first part of the book deals with the practical tasks of shaping and planting the garden to be a multipurpose landscape asset and yet yield cut flowers for indoor bouquets without defacing itself. Much of this information will be familiar to those already experienced in working with plants, soil, and the elements, and who have a basic grasp on how these interact. But I am putting my faith in Thomas Jefferson's remark, "Though an old man, I am still but a young gardener," and trust that these pages will hold something for the advanced gardener as well as the novice, specifically from the viewpoint of turning the entire home landscape into a garden for cutting.

I should point out that my 20 years of gardening have been carried on in that part of New York which falls into Zone 6 on the USDA hardiness map, and the plants mentioned in this book are hardy at least to this zone, unless stated otherwise. Readers who garden in other parts of the country will have to generalize from my experience and complement it with information appropriate to their own region; suggestions are offered in the Bibliography.

The final part of the book deals with creating indoor bouquets and is, to borrow from Robert Browning, "the last for which the first began." It is guided by the philosophy that anyone who takes the time and trouble to grow flowers for cutting is entitled to the simple happiness of bringing them indoors and displaying them without a lot of fuss. If the term "flower arranging" is intimidating to those who have never put flowers together in a vase,

consider that flower arranging can, in fact, be practiced on any level. In arrangements, taste—a quality that grows and changes—can run from untutored charm to unabashed opulence. With this in mind, I have included tips gleaned over the years from talented experts as well as those learned from my own experience. They are offered as a springboard for those with little practice to take courage and begin to develop

their individual style. Perhaps they will also remind the more advanced arranger of a few forgotten details.

I am a firm believer that "experience is a good school, but only fools will know no other." We learn from each other and in many ways, as well as from our own mistakes and successes. My hope is that this book will bring more joy to your gardening, and more flowers into your house.

TAKING
STOCK

ABOVE *A wire basket entwined with ivy and
filled with lilacs, Dutch irises, peonies, and
baby rosebuds gleaned from the garden make a
lovely table decoration for a
June wedding.*

FACING PAGE *Using treasured possessions,
such as this collection of china, to hold favorite
garden flowers enhances each, and doubles the
pleasure they give.*

PAGES 12–13 *Gomphrena for drying,
Sedum 'Autumn Joy', asters, goldenrod, and
cosmos are only part of the fall bounty offered
by this country garden north of
New York City.*

PAGE 13 *Peonies carry their own weight
and loveliness in bouquets—nothing more
is needed.*

To pick flowers from the garden and bring them indoors is a natural extension of flower gardening. And to have a garden provide flowers for the house when you want them for indoor bouquets, in colors and shapes of your choosing, adds a new dimension to gardening.

The aim is not to gather hit or miss a few humble though breathtaking bunches to strike an occasional note of cheer in the daily routine, desirable as that is. The ideal is to cultivate an abundance of flowers—a continuity of blossoms and leaves. Let them bedeck a corner cupboard, the mantelpiece, bookshelf, or sofa table—any of those special niches that demand flowers lest the room seem somehow uninhabited. The intention is to live with fresh garden flowers in spring, summer, and fall, and to improvise with berries, branches, and greenery—dried flowers, too—until spring comes again.

Gardens, even those lacking a vegetable plot, are by and large decorative and functional. They are places where we can relax, entertain, and dream in pleasant settings fash-

ioned to suit our life-style. Flower beds and borders, however, serve primarily as ornaments—as the centerpieces of the garden, rather than main sources of flowers for the dining table. (For simplicity, "bed" and "border" are used interchangeably in this book. Traditionally a border refers to a long rectangular planting, containing mostly perennials, that flows along the property line, or borders a walk or lawn and is backed by a hedge, fence, wall, or building.) Similarly, we expect background trees, shrubs, ground covers, and ornamental grasses to put a good face on our home ground, and cutting from them for indoor displays might spoil the landscape. To make the garden practical for cutting without compromising its beauty is a challenge.

To realize this dream is not so much a matter of increasing the investment of time, effort, and money spent on the garden. It is mainly adopting a different mind-set—gardening with a "cutting point of view," so to speak—and exercising that viewpoint by planning and planting with bouquets in mind: bouquets not just from the flower

LEFT *Exuberant hollyhocks grow among masses of colorful flowers, perfectly reflecting the informal architecture of this French farmhouse in California. The owner is gradually replacing water-thirsty plants with drought-resistant perennials.*

RIGHT *Blooms of tree peonies make exquisite cut flowers, whether they are displayed in a cut-crystal vase or in a country jug, as they are here in the author's garden. Tree peonies (*Paeonia suffruticosa*) are easy-care shrubs that bloom earlier than herbaceous peonies.*

garden, but from the entire home landscape with its background plantings of trees and shrubs, its ground covers, vines, herbs, and even vegetables. It means thinking about your arranging needs and rethinking your style of gardening, of selecting plants that are vase-worthy as well as garden-worthy, and choosing plants with assets for two or even three seasons of interest. It means thrifty use of growing space—especially for small gardens—to assure plenty of flowers for the house throughout the growing season. This applies whether you are planning a new landscape or making major changes in an outgrown one. Any well-established garden can be easily modified to accommodate plants valuable for cutting.

Most gardens lend themselves to two main approaches for supplying cut flowers for the house. One is to adapt the flower border (or borders) to serve as both a decorative feature and a main source for cut flowers; the other route is to create a separate cutting garden in which flowers are grown exclusively for making bouquets. (Gardens in which every square foot of space counts might hold both a small cutting garden and a double-duty border to produce the quantity of flowers wanted.) In either case, the rest of the landscape should yield light pickings to supplement the main supply.

The garden proper plays an

essential supporting role. It has the potential to round out your bouquets with additional flowers and foliage, and provide branches, evergreen foliage, and colorful berries and leaves during the months when flowers are scarce or absent. (Even modest and ubiquitous ground covers such as ajuga, periwinkle, and pachysandra can be put to many uses indoors; garnish a bowl of lemons and limes with sprigs of pachysandra, or tuck ajuga into a basket of miniature gourds and pumpkins to capture an autumnal mood for a lunch or buffet.)

Most gardens, even the smallest, traditionally contain a decorative border, which is turned to when flowers are wanted for the house. Too often, however, when flowers are wanted, the following scenario occurs: gardener wanders into the garden, shears in hand, stands indecisive before the flower border—which is looking quite pretty at last—and returns empty-handed to the house. Or only a handful of blooms is picked with a disquieting feeling that Peter is being robbed to pay Paul. This unhappy outcome is avoidable, though.

By focusing one's planning—and deviating slightly from conventional wisdom in the planting stage—it's possible to create a double-duty border that will yield plenty of flowers and foliage for cutting and still look attractive. This is a tall order, and to pull it off requires careful planning, dedication, physical effort, and a dose of garden "smarts." But it is

also a joyous and rewarding challenge, as long as it is understood there is no such thing as instant gratification in gardening.

At first, it might seem that the main advantage to adapting the display border as a cutting bed is that you will not have to create and maintain a separate garden from which to cut flowers. Actually, the easiest, most sensible way to have armloads of nonstop flowers for bouquets is to grow them in a separate cutting garden. Because a proper cutting garden is hidden away in the landscape, it can become your secret garden, where you can indulge your horticultural likes and dislikes, be innovative and productive, learn and grow along with your plants. It does not have to be large to be productive. It can be any size you and your garden can accommodate. The only unbreakable rule is that the cutting garden be set apart visually from the rest of your garden.

I strongly favor a cutting garden as the main provider of cut flowers. It best suits my temperament, my needs, and my garden (two acres of hilly land about 35 miles north of New York City). Even so, I arrived at this solution only after years of filching flowers, with sinking heart, from my small twin borders next to the terrace. I created one small cutting garden, about 15 feet by 15 feet, near the compost pile, and in it I grow mostly annuals, a few biennials, tulips, and dahlias. I built another cutting garden behind a wall on top of a slope to hold

those essential classics that never fail to inject a note of romance and nostalgia in an arrangement—peonies, irises, lilies, delphiniums—as well as a few dependable, long-blooming daisies. Thanks to my cutting gardens, I have been able to fill our house with jugs of colorful flowers whenever I like, from spring to fall, and still have plenty of extras to take to our city friends. This brings them and me enormous pleasure and is reason enough to maintain a cutting garden.

Begin by thinking seriously about how much time and energy you are willing and able to devote to gardening. Juggling demands of family, career, and community often leaves precious little time for gardening, sports, or other interests. It is perhaps gratuitous, but still worth repeating, to say that you should take on only as much gardening as you can handle solo or with regular help, as the case may be.

Also, although it may sound frivolous to suggest that you consider your personality when planning a garden, it is not farfetched to do so (as the garden writer and TV personality Thalassa Cruso pointed out so sensibly years ago in *Making Things Grow Outdoors*). Aside from other benefits, gardening should be a way of unfettering yourself from daily stress, not adding to it. If you are meticulous about your house and dress, perhaps, paradoxically, you would be better off with an informal garden—one in which a degree of disarray is acceptable and not a call

to bring out rake or pruning shears to set things right.

By contrast, if your temperament tends toward the easygoing and casual, a formal garden might be your best choice. Neatly laid out beds would restrain gay, careless masses of flowers, and you could enjoy both the freewheeling planting and an ordered basic design. Take a few moments to mull over this matter. Respecting your inherent makeup and working with it will increase the pleasure you derive from your garden and, in the long run, produce better results.

Whether you opt for a cutting garden or double-duty border to meet your arranging needs, it is a good idea to spend some time sorting out these needs. Flower arrangements can range from those unstructured bunches that exuberantly defy every rule and all logic and yet bring so much pleasure, to sophisticated creations that are

LEFT *Plants with handsome foliage are coveted for the garden and for arranging. The burgundy foliage of* Heuchera *'Palace Purple' is even more striking when juxtaposed with the finely cut blue-gray foliage of* Ruta graveolens *'Jackman's Blue'. They are seen here in the display garden at Heronswood Nursery, in Kingston, Washington.*

FACING PAGE *The "English" roses bunched here have the old-fashioned look and fragrance of antique shrub roses, but they are modern hybrids that bloom all summer. Included are The Squire, a velvety crimson rose, Fair Bianca, white; and Mary Rose, a rich pink, with a few shell pink blooms of the lovely climbing rose New Dawn.*

hands-down blue-ribbon candidates, and include everything in between.

Think about the times you habitually want bouquets. Do you like to keep a centerpiece or a row of bud vases on the dining table, the kitchen counter, the vanity, or the desk in your home office? Perhaps you keep a large urn or brass scuttle on the fireplace hearth, as I do, filling it according to the season with flowering or berried branches and tawny ornamental grasses. (Placing a large display on the floor in this way allows you to keep to scale when a room is small or has a low ceiling.)

What holidays, birthdays, and anniversaries do you celebrate that would be incomplete without flowers? Do you entertain often, going all out with flowers when you do? Are there other special occasions that you want to honor with flowers, such as a birth or graduation? Perhaps your flower arrangements are widely admired, and friends have asked you to make the bouquets or

pew markers for a wedding or for church services; fresh flowers from your garden would be an especially personal contribution. Weighing these matters will give you a rough idea of the quantities of flowers you want, and of how busy you will be. Are your expectations realistic?

There is no arguing that fresh flowers are decorative, and they will enhance a room as nothing else can. If you are an ardent arranger, with an eye for design, it will help to study the rooms in which you want to place flowers. Then you can plan to grow them in the colors and shapes that will carry out your decorating scheme. This is not to say, however, that you will have exactly the flowers and foliage you want for a particular occasion a year hence. In this case adopt a pragmatic philosophy: plan diligently, but assume the unexpected will happen. The white lilies you ordered will bloom in tangerine orange; the delphiniums will perish from unknown causes;

campanulas will be late to bloom, or early; woodchucks or deer will strip the flower beds, and your own tastes and plans may change. Proceeding in good faith is all you can do; if the modicum of extra attention paid results in a few fabulous bouquets for special occasions, the pleasure will be worth it.

Novice as well as advanced arrangers can visualize whether a space calls for a dramatic, assertive display of large flowers and sculptural branches or less imposing, beguiling bouquets and charming posies. Note background colors, textures, and patterns of curtains, wallpaper, rugs, and nearby upholstery fabrics. Study how the colors change in different lighting such as candlelight or incandescent. Flowers come in almost every imaginable hue, tint, and shade, which can be matched or contrasted with your room decorations. If your overall dining or living room color scheme is in soft, salmony peach shades, for example, daylilies, snapdragons, and some roses come in colors that would blend perfectly; for a little more punch, mix flowers in soft blues, yellows, and cream. Search catalogs and nurseries for the flowers you want, and make notes to record your thoughts.

Gardens present panoramic views; indoor bouquets give us close-ups. Aside from size and color, when selecting plants look for traits that would be assets when seen up close in an arrangement but which often go unnoticed in the garden. Some of the markings on petals are masterpieces

of design—primulas, fully opened tulips, and the faces of pansies. The anthers of poppies, lilies, and many other flowers are highly decorative. Petals can be frilly, pinked, smooth, double, single, and so on. Notice their texture—satiny, papery, coarse—which affects how they reflect light in a bouquet. The varying forms and shapes of flowers and florets include the open faces of daisies, cups, bells, pendants, spikes, and plates. The richness of detail is seemingly endless. Sensitizing yourself to it will soon become a habit that will enrich your bouquets.

While in this exploratory phase, give a few thoughts to your favorite containers, the ones that set the tone for the kinds of flowers you will put in them. For instance, a branch or two of white dogwood blossoms (perhaps the shrubby, white-flowering *Cornus alba* 'Sibirica') might add just the right touch of elegance to a silver Art Deco vase, and vice versa, as would lilacs in shades of pink and purple, as well as white. Consider *Lavatera thuringiaca* 'Barnsley' for the majolica pitcher you carried back from Italy; the silky pink chalicelike blooms will pick up the pitcher's lavender tints for a dreamy melding of flowers and container—and the lavatera's blossoms and lush green leaves stay fresh for several days.

As for longevity: while the blooms of some plants will last a long time in a vase of water, others are notoriously short-lived. Experience and the information in the Plant Profiles will help you to identify which are

which. Other factors affect a flower's vase life as well. Such matters as the time of day you cut them, their stage in their bloom cycle, and how you condition and refresh them after they've been arranged in a bouquet are important, and in some cases, critical. (See pages 120–126.)

If you have only a few flowers to play with, naturally you'll want to stretch out their life span as long as possible. But longevity is less crucial for home gardeners than for commercial cut-flower growers and florists. Gardeners can afford to be extravagant with flowers, especially when a cutting garden is supplying the flowers. We have the privilege, if we wish to use it, of indulging in really fresh garden bouquets and replacing blooms the moment they flag. (If you harbor guilt feelings about waste—and even if you don't—toss the remains on the compost pile to be recycled.) Many old roses are ravishing but erratically short-lived after they are cut. These include the gallicas, damasks, moss roses, and other antique kinds. (The hybrid teas, which I find too stiff for arrangements in any case, and the grandifloras and other modern roses do not have this shortcoming.) Blooms of pink-and-white-striped Rosa Mundi, heady Felicité Parmentier, the artist's rose Fantin-Latour, or elegant white Madame Hardy (to mention only a few) make a gorgeous centerpiece for a dinner party or for supper on a quiet evening. They last only the night, but while they do they provide a memorable magic.

Most seasoned gardeners will agree that nothing is more important than assessing every square foot of your land so you know it intimately before you landscape the grounds. Even if you have an established garden and think you know its character, look at it again with fresh eyes until you uncover all its secrets. Study it over the seasons, a year at least. Take your time; make notes. Walk it with your family, gardening friends, and alone; know it at sunrise and at sunset and in all kinds of weather. Study the way the light strikes it; learn where the wind blows and from which direction (some plants will dry out and die in persistent winds), and if there are protected microclimates. Determine if the soil is sandy or boggy, if it is acidic or alkaline (best to take a sample to your county extension office for a soil test), and whether there is a problem with rocky ledges or an eyesore.

It's critical to know the weather and climate conditions of your region and the hardiness zone you garden in so you can choose plants to withstand your winters. (See the USDA Plant Hardiness Zone Map, revised in 1990, at the end of this book.) An experienced gardener in your neighborhood can be a valuable source of information on local plant hardiness; don't be timid about asking for advice, as most gardeners are willing to oblige.

Intimate familiarity with your property will be the basis for your garden making. Apply to your garden Alexander Pope's dictum to

ABOVE *Treillage and shrubs provide an attractive background for a border in a Connecticut garden that melds formal and informal elements. The hard edging keeps plants and lawn from encroaching on one another, and the massed planting softens the effect.*

BELOW *For those occasions when a large arrangement is wanted, plan to include at least one showy cultivar of* Phlox paniculata, *and grow it in the border or clumped in front of background shrubs. The pyramidal flower clusters of sprightly 'Bright Eyes' make a bold statement in late summer, cut or uncut.*

"consult the Genius of the place in all," for that is the issue: to uncover the special qualities of your property—the lay of the land, its stone, earth, water, air, and light—even the landscape and architecture surrounding it. Then you can take advantage of your "givens" by turning a boulder-strewn slope into a rock garden, a boggy area into a water garden, a shaded area into a serene green garden free from clocks, telephones, and television. Create a garden that belongs, that respects today's environmental concerns, that reflects you and your life-style—and one that is generous enough to fill your life with its flowery bounty. Most of all, savor every stage of its creation, which can span a lifetime.

STARTING
WITH THE
LANDSCAPE

Garden Design

Woody Plants

ABOVE *Branches of an apple tree in bloom are lovely against the sky or in a vase.*

FACING PAGE *A solid landscape design is the basis for an attractive, livable garden. Trees and shrubs provide background structure and enclosure, a vine-shaded terrace conveniently close to the house creates a sitting and dining area, and a circuitous path through the flower garden invites a stroll among the billowing colors, textures, and shapes. One of the owners, a painter and creative flower arranger, picks from the garden shown here, as well as from a small cutting garden.*

PAGES 22–23 *Ground covers of hostas and daylilies spill over a Virginia hillside garden.*

PAGE 23 *Flower plumes and dark burgundy foliage of smokebush (*Cotinus coggygria*) highlight the daisylike heads of purple cone-flower (*Echinacea purpurea*), inspiring a similar pairing in a bouquet.*

The term "garden," aside from referring to a food garden, used to mean a place to walk through, a place to be looked at rather than to be lived in. We still want to look at our gardens, to enjoy the richness of forms, shapes, textures, and color, but today that is not their only function.

A dramatic change in American garden style began in California during the 1930s and 1940s with the gardens designed by the late Thomas Church. As smaller houses became popular and indoor living space dwindled, Church saw the simple logic of melding the house with the garden, of extending indoor activities into the outdoors. His philosophy is summed up in the title of his widely read book, *Gardens Are for People.*

Today, our gardens reflect this influence. The terrace and the garden closest to the house relate to the interior. They provide places for shelling peas, tinkering with the bike, entertaining, and lounging. But gardens differ markedly, being shaped by the diverse climate and growing conditions of various regions across the country, not to mention local social and gardening traditions and individual life-styles. The urge to engage in the ancient pleasures of digging, planting, smelling, touching, and strolling in our gardens runs strong. Nothing less than a true garden will satisfy—one with grass, trees and shrubs, vegetable plots, herb gardens, wildflower meadows, and flower gardens.

Since the 1960s, a growing concern about the natural environment has also influenced gardening. Increasingly dangerous demands are being placed on natural resources, and the fact that water is not an inexhaustible resource has become alarmingly clear. People living where rainfall is scarce are learning to live with water restrictions, and the focus is on using drought-resistant native plants and ornamental grasses in gardens. In many parts of the country, traditional lawns and flower borders are giving way to sweeps of undemanding grasses, perennial wildflowers, and native woody plants.

We are appreciating more and more the virtues of native plants and learning how best to use them in our

ABOVE *Willow-leaved helianthus (Helianthus salicifolius) blooms against a stable in late September in North Salem, New York. Plants that bloom heavily late in the season are valuable to the arranger, and can be planted in clumps away from the main garden.*

FACING PAGE, TOP *A front garden in the suburbs of Chicago planted with daylilies, pink phlox, and loosestrife spills out into the street to welcome visitors. Flowers from the beds here and elsewhere in the garden are used in weekly altar arrangements for the owner's church.*

FACING PAGE, BOTTOM *Another Chicago garden, designed by Craig Bergman and James Grigsby, offers a pergola entwined with honeysuckle and a bench for reading— or for contemplating the rubrum lilies, pink and blue larkspur, and low-growing plants which flank the path.*

gardens. These are the plants whose forebears are the species that grow wild in the fields and woodlands, prairies and deserts. They have survived by adapting to local soils and climates, making them dependable and undemanding plants for gardens. They blend easily with each other, harmonize the garden with surrounding nature, and reduce maintenance. In bouquets, they offer an appealing insouciance. Native plants are worth seeking out, but they should be purchased only from nurseries known to propagate their own wildflowers. Those who pillage from the wild endanger species and their habitats. Local and national wildflower groups are a good source of information. (See also the listing in the Sources.)

Because a home garden is our personal dominion, a really good garden will hold something of our spirit and personality. It will reflect our needs, style, and tastes, whether we revel in clutter or order. As much as we dote on flowers, they are, admittedly, only part (alas, usually the smallest part) of the larger garden picture. The larger scene, our landscape, must also accommodate other needs and pleasures. Before we fill it with flowers and foliage, we must first organize it to accomplish all that we expect of it.

Garden Design

Goethe is supposed to have said that a garden is made not from a plan but from a feeling heart. Despite the underlying wisdom, there can be no harm in backing up the heart's desires with a practical plan. For most of us, a "designed" garden—one that has been thought through and whose choices are intentional—will be more satisfying than one that evolves piecemeal as inspiration strikes. And it is not insignificant that thoughtful planning saves time and money in the long run.

Not everybody will be making a fresh start. Some will want to remodel a mature garden or one that comes with a "new" home. Others may already have a well-loved garden and simply want to strengthen its cutting potential. Sometimes, a judicious thinning and pruning of overgrown trees to open vistas and let in more sunlight and air circulation for flower beds will be the only facelift some gardens need. If you have inherited somebody else's garden, spend a full year observing what pops out of the ground before making changes; it would be a pity to dig up inadvertently a ten-year-old peony bed or a hillside of daffodils or daylilies.

Designing or remodeling a landscape falls within the creative capabilities of home owners with a will to do it. While it requires a great deal of research and careful analysis, it can also be fun; involve family members and even close friends who will share their ideas (and mistakes) with you.

If you now own a new home and are literally working from scratch, surrounded with builder's rubble, or if you must solve major problems

with drainage or slope grading, it would be prudent and perhaps necessary to bring in professional help. What you choose to do yourself and what you have others do for you depends on your interest, skills, time, energy, and budget. If you can find a good landscape architect who will work on a consulting basis, your money would be well spent. Few can have an ideal landscape right away, but time is on your side. After you have completed a final design for your property, the most satisfying way to proceed is by stages, completing one project before beginning another. This will give you the opportunity to correct or learn from mistakes. Living with your unfinished landscape will clarify your needs so you can fine-tune your plans as you go along.

In the interim, you needn't deprive yourself of a prelude to things to come. After the spring thaw, as soon as the soil is dry enough to work, find a sunny area near the house where you can dig out a small temporary flower bed (add organic material to the soil) where you can plant easy colorful annuals—cosmos, cleomes, bachelor's-buttons, nasturtiums, marigolds, snapdragons, and zinnias. If you are really eager, begin seeds indoors of some fast-growing perennials that will bloom their first year if started in early spring—Starburst shasta daisy, Early Sunrise coreopsis, and golden marguerite (*Anthemis tinctoria* 'Kelwayi'). This will give you something cheerful to look out on and to bring

into the house for summer bunches. The flower bed will have paid its way by fall, and you can abandon or expand it the following year. You can also draw on this initial experience in planning your future flower beds and indoor arrangements.

Early on, you should have some idea of what mood you want your garden to reflect. This will give it coherence and also affect subsequent furnishings, materials, and plants. There are two dominant styles,

ABOVE *A curtain of climbing ivy and white Clematis 'Henryi' conceal all but the roof of a teahouse, designed by Innocenti in the 1940s as a focal point in this Massachusetts garden. Mountain laurel (Kalmia sp.), bleeding-heart, lamb's-ears, lady's-mantle, and white phlox adorn its base.*

FACING PAGE *A steep slope has been woven into a tapestry of flowers and foliage in this garden outside of Seattle designed by Dan Borroff. Featured here are white Phlox maculata 'Miss Lingard' and P. paniculata 'Everest', pink Astilbe × arendsii 'Erica', Campanula lactiflora 'Pouffe', alstroemeria, roses, and ornamental grasses.*

formal and informal. Formal style is characterized by straight lines, geometic shapes, and symmetry. It is tidy, neat, and requires high maintenance. An informal style is achieved by curving lines that flow along the landscape and asymmetrical balance in which a colorful flower border on one side of a door can be balanced by a larger, all-green planting on the other. It evokes a casual mood, but not sloppiness. Either formal or informal landscape styles will complement a formally designed house, but an informal style is called for where the land is hilly or irregular and the architecture informal. Ideally, the landscape closest to the house should be compatible with the style and colors inside the house.

While it's useful to review the characteristics of each style, there's no need to become tied up in knots about which style to follow. The best gardens are often a graceful combination of elements of each. Experts often start with a simple, uncluttered plan for the outdoor space, which can then be softened by luxuriant plantings spilling over straight lines and hard surfaces. When deciding your particular style, think about how it will fit into both natural surroundings and regional tradition. In the end, however, it is your property, and you should please yourself and your own informed taste.

Clarify what you need and what you want in the preliminary stages. Take a long and earnest look at how the lot will be used and what your priorities are. First consider the front garden and approach to your home, which sets the tone. Many home owners are breaking away from the traditional front yard of lawn, evergreen shrubs, and a tree or two. Flower borders, modified meadows with ornamental grasses, and vegetables (many are highly decorative) are beginning to come out of hiding at the back of the house to tumble from the front door to the street in innovative, attractive ways. No doubt you have to accommodate a driveway and allow for parking as unobtrusively as possible but in a convenient area. You will also have to determine how to link the separate areas with paths and walks for easy traffic flow; consider laying them along the route you normally take while traversing the lot, as that is presumably the most natural and comfortable way to proceed.

Begin by drawing to scale a base map of your house and property, including boundaries, utility lines, drainspouts, existing trees or plantings, paths, driveway, and so on. If you have a survey map, deed, or house plan, it will spare you hours of work and measuring. Use this base map, overlaid with tracing paper at first, to try out your ideas for the design. The aim is to organize and shape the property to accommodate the different use areas—for welcome, recreation, work, storage—and beautiful gardens.

As your layout progresses, you will use many sheets of tracing paper over your base map as you fiddle with design ideas. Study the design

away from the drawing board, visualizing how different views, structures, and plantings will look from windows and doors inside the house as well as while meandering over the lot.

Consciously or not, while designing the landscape you will be dealing with basic artistic principles such as simplicity, unity, proportion, balance, and harmony. These apply to all good garden design, whether you are planning a terrace, flower bed, or indoor arrangement. These principles are concepts rather than rules. They are hard-to-define qualities whose presence we note subconsciously, and we are aware that something is amiss when they are lacking. Use them as guidelines to test your ideas.

Decide which areas of new planting are necessary and how to fit them into your garden according to good design principles. Shapes, height, and bulk are important at this point; choosing specific plants comes later.

Trees are of first importance, then shrubs. Massed plantings of trees and shrubs will shelter and frame the garden, provide screening and privacy where you want it, define boundaries, and provide shade in summer. Evergreens will buffer the effects of wind to insulate the house in winter and filter out street noises. The larger specimen trees—only one or two if your garden is small—will also be the linchpins to tie the house to the garden, and to carry your eye through the garden to the landscape beyond.

Plan the flower beds for sunny spots with good drainage, if possible.

Where there is shade, a green garden primarily of shrubs, hostas, and ferns can be restful; if color is wanted, choose perennials and annuals that tolerate or even require some shade. In small gardens, a space in the angle of the house, beside a terrace, or to the side of the lawn may call out for flowers. Such spaces will act as "bouquets" in your garden rather than as a main source of pickings for your indoor arrangements. Other possible sites for flower beds are along the front of the house, against an evergreen hedge, or in front of shrubs at the verges of the property. A mixed border of shrubs and flowers placed at some distance from the house can contribute to your indoor bouquets; the holes caused by cutting will be scarcely noticeable and will not detract from the overall colorful display.

It's important, especially on large properties, that flower beds and borders not look randomly placed. They should be somehow connected to another architectural feature or display or else separate other parts of the garden from each other. A wall, fence, or hedge can enclose a flower garden or combination cutting-vegetable garden. A hedge, maybe a soft-needled, luxuriantly green yew, can act as the background for a border on one side while hiding a cutting garden on the other. Island beds can be placed on the lawn like colorful jewels, to be walked around and admired from all sides. (One sizable island bed, however, generally will be more effective visually than two smaller ones; and

mowing the surrounding lawn will be easier.)

Many excellent books deal with the details of the multifaceted discipline of landscape design. They include construction techniques for terraces, decks, paths, walls, water gardens, and so on, and discuss garden design and planting schemes. (See Bibliography.)

After you have settled on a design, it is time to select plants, which will supply the missing elements—nature's vitality and beauty—and transform your property into a garden. This is a wonderful opportunity to plan and plant a new property with cutting in mind. If your garden is already well established, it is relatively easy to add new plants with the colors and qualities you want for arrangements.

Woody Plants

The long-lasting woody plants, trees and shrubs, have overlapping characteristics and uses, and are the first to be planted. They give the garden its permanent structure and furnishings, making them long-term investments. Woody plants can be deciduous or evergreen; evergreen trees and shrubs can be either needled (the conifers) or broad-leaved, such as hollies and rhododendrons. Many produce handsome berries and leaf color, so their usefulness spans the year. They are remarkably practical and decorative on the landscape, and a few cut branches will bring the seasons' moods into the house as nothing else can. That they

ABOVE *A central walk brings a sense of order to garden writer Linda Yang's teeming garden behind a brownstone in the heart of New York City.*

FACING PAGE, TOP *A brick path gracefully unites the flower beds in this Virginia garden as it winds past warm-colored daylilies in the foreground to purple coneflowers and buddleia in the back.*

FACING PAGE, MIDDLE *Handsome masonry divides a California garden, designed by Thomas Church, into separate areas. Strong, primarily straight lines and the symmetry of the double flower borders set a formal mood.*

FACING PAGE, BOTTOM *An unobstructed view across a lake is enhanced by the bountiful plantings of long-blooming (and cuttable) marguerite daisies and other annuals in containers built into the terrace.*

PAGES 36–37 *Spring is captured in garden writer Sydney Eddison's Connecticut garden by clumps of cream and white Darwin tulips, daffodils, and yellow* Draba sibirica *in the border, and reinforced by a weeping cherry tree and the dainty double white blossoms of* Prunus × *'Hally Jolivette'.*

also require little maintenance makes them almost too good to be true.

The distinctions between trees and shrubs are somewhat vague and artificial. Some woody plants straddle the line between tall shrubs and small trees, depending on growing conditions and how they are pruned. Generally shrubs are looked upon as woody plants with multiple trunks or stems that grow no higher than 15 or 20 feet. They can be used in greater numbers than trees in smaller

gardens. Most grow fairly quickly and begin paying returns early. Trees are bigger, often single-trunked, and usually take longer to grow to maturity than shrubs. If your property already holds a few mature trees, consider them the living capital of your garden; they can increase real estate values markedly.

TREES

Although major landscape investments such as trees are not selected

from the perspective of vase-worthiness—the first consideration is their intended function on the landscape—they can contribute splendid raw material to be turned into indoor arrangements. The situation is most favorable when a tree is intended primarily as an ornamental; then the same features that make it a pleasing attraction outdoors will translate easily into refreshing indoor displays. Avoid cutting extravagantly or helter-skelter from a tree; you'll be left with a lopsided effect that will take nature a long time to correct (if at all). Also, as immature trees continue to grow, you may need long-handled loppers, a ladder series, and, quite possibly, the agility to shinny up a tree's limbs to reach the desired blooms, foliage, or berries.

Whether selecting evergreen or deciduous trees, shop wisely. First choose only those cultivars that are known to grow well in the climate and soil conditions of your garden. Talk to experienced gardeners in your neighborhood and seek advice from a reliable local nursey. It would be expensive and wasteful, never mind disappointing, to lose, say, a *Magnolia grandiflora* that is reliably hardy only to Zone 7 in your Zone 5 Ohio garden.

Consider the size and shape that will do the best job for the place and purpose it is to fill. Trees range in size from small to towering, in shapes that are rounded, pyramidal, vaselike, cloudlike, fan-shaped, or upright, and each has something special to offer. Do you want dense,

heavy shade such as a Norway maple will provide or the light, airy effect and profusion of spring blossoms of a graceful serviceberry? Remember that grass and flowers will not grow under trees that cast heavy shade; even when light is ample, many plants cannot compete with the greedy tree roots of a beech or maple. If you want deciduous spring-flowering trees, plant at least one so you can enjoy it from your favorite lookout in the house.

Find out the mature height and spread of each serious candidate, and how fast it will grow. Will it stay in bounds and not infringe on the street, house, or another tree? Otherwise, branches of a prized linden, planted next to the house as a shade tree, may someday dangerously overhang the roof; an eight-foot blue spruce, planted too close to the front walk, will encroach on the walk and pedestrians as it grows toward its full height of perhaps 60 feet and a 20-foot spread. Ignore these matters and in the end you may have to call in costly professional help to prune or remove the tree.

In another instance, you may want a fast-growing tree to disguise a telephone pole. It will help the decision-making process to know that the pyramid-shaped katsura tree (*Cercidiphyllum japonicum*) will grow quickly to 25 feet in several years, then settle into a slower pace until it reaches its full 40 to 60 feet. Its astonishing foliage—heart-shaped leaves, blood red in spring, blue-green in summer, and yellow and red in fall—is re-

markably disease- and pest-free. Cut its twigs for forcing; the young leaves will unfurl indoors to add ruby-red accents to spring bunches.

You will also want to know about the structural soundness of the tree you are considering, especially in areas of high wind and winters with freezing rain and snow. Again, the nursery where you are buying your tree can supply this information. Supplement this by buying a comprehensive tree encyclopedia. (See Bibliography.)

Evergreen trees, both conifers and broad-leaved, impart a timeless calm to the garden with their year-round presence. They bring color to the bleak winter landscape, and in summer they make a cool green backdrop for a chorus of flowering shrubs and perennials. Nothing is more satisfying than the December ritual of bundling up on a raw morning and going out into one's own backyard to cut armloads of red berries and fresh greens that scent the air with resin. Boxwood, yew, holly, fir, pine, and juniper can be gleaned from my garden for Christmas decorations, though I cut selectively. The broad-leaved evergreens are invigorated by pruning; the conifers are fast growers, but most—pines, spruces, firs, and cypresses, for instance—do not replenish their cut limbs.

Conifers are the tallest evergreens in the North. There are more than 550 different species spread over the earth. They carry their seeds in woody cones, which are often ornamental and popular for making

ABOVE *A view toward the wilder parts of a garden on Bainbridge Island, Washington, emphasizes the beauty, structure, and variety that trees and shrubs can bring to the landscape. Woody plants also provide a diversity of materials for cutting, including foliage in wonderful colors, such as the burgundy leaves of shrubby purple hazel under the weeping willow tree. Vines, perennials, and annuals planted at the base create casual, appealing borders that offer additional pickings for bouquets.*

FACING PAGE *A whimsical yew topiary, encircled by boxwood, makes an amusing focal point in front of a hedge of clipped hemlock in the Virginia countryside. Topiaries and formally shaped hedges require regular clipping. Sheared hedges are superb for dividing a garden into "rooms," and they provide effective backgrounds for flower beds.*

wreaths, swags, and indoor decorations. They have their own problems with pests and diseases, but otherwise are relatively care-free. Best of all, perhaps, no leaf-raking is needed, although they drop and replace their needles periodically. A few cut branchlets of a soft-needled conifer such as white pine make a graceful winter arrangement mingled in a vase with a spray or two of small florists' orchids (and will last almost indefinitely). Most conifers grow naturally in geometric shapes, columnar or conical, creating strong accents that seldom need pruning. Use narrow upright conifers with restraint; too many on a small landscape can create a restless staccato mood.

A row of sheared hemlocks (*Tsuga* spp.), arborvitaes (*Thuja* spp., some forms of which are grown as shrubs), or red cedars (*Juniperus virginiana*) can be planted as a year-round screen between your property and adjacent properties or the road, or to block out an eyesore. Such screening is practical, effective, and depending on the size of the purchased plants, relatively inexpensive in the long run. For a focal point, a single Colorado blue spruce is often (too often, really) used as the icy prima donna of the garden; other stars include false cypresses (*Chamaecyparis* spp.), true cedars (*Cedrus* spp.), and fast-growing white pines. Cedars are majestic when mature and show off best in a large setting, but many are slow-growing. The weeping blue Atlas cedar (*Cedrus atlantica* 'Glauca Pendula') is particularly lovely; a single

foot-long snipping of its silvery blue drooping branchlets will provide an exciting focal point for a modern arrangement.

Junipers play many roles in the garden, from thick, year-round carpeting to tall, impressive accents. There are many kinds, suitable for virtually every type of climate across the country; they like the sun, but a few (very few), such as the Pfitzer juniper, will tolerate moderate shade. As is true of other needled "evergreens," junipers are not all green; some cultivars (cultivated varieties) come in shades of gray, blue, bronze, or gold. Snippings of their densely needled branches can be used as fillers in flower displays; their tightly packed grayish blue berries are as useful for winter arrangements as they are for making gin.

Tall broad-leaved evergreen trees are most suited to warm climates. The queen among broad-leaved evergreens is the stately southern magnolia (*Magnolia grandiflora*, z 7–9), spectacular in form (to 80 feet), with fragrant blossoms (12–14 inches across) and gleaming leaves. It needs mild winters or a protected site, perhaps against a north-facing wall, out of the winter sun. New varieties are being developed for colder climates; the cultivars 'Timeless Beauty' and 'Edith Bogue' are said to be marginally hardy, with winter protection, along the coast up to New Hampshire.

The deciduous saucer magnolia (*M. × soulangiana*) is a welcome consolation prize for those who cannot

ABOVE *The magnificent saucer-shaped flowers of saucer magnolia tree (*Magnolia × soulangiana*) may reach ten inches in diameter when they are fully open, at times remaining on the tree until the leaves unfold.*

FACING PAGE *A 60-year-old saucer magnolia tree framing an old well in a Connecticut garden has reached its mature height of about 30 feet. Saucer magnolias are hardy to Zone 4, but if the flower buds are nipped by a late spring frost, they will not bloom.*

flowers, silver-backed foliage, and dark red showy fruit; it grows rapidly, is not fussy about sunlight, and will even adjust to swampy soil. I grow the cultivar 'Rosea' (pink buds open to white) of the star magnolia on a slope under a weeping cherry tree, which blooms at about the same time (usually in early April). Pink cherry blossoms overhang the white ribbony star flowers of the magnolia, making a pretty picture from both the living room window and front road. Magnolia flowers combined in a vase with the cherry blossoms, a few tulips, daffodils, or sprays of bleeding-heart make for a lovely spring arrangement.

If you decide that your landscape is incomplete without a member of this ancient clan (debates rage about whether the magnolia is our planet's oldest flower), remember this: when planting a magnolia, set it in the soil at the exact level that it was growing at the nursery; planting too deeply is the single most common cause of the early demise of most trees, but none more so than the magnolia.

Along with the broad-leaved evergreens, flowering deciduous trees, too, bring incomparable seasonal beauty to the homesite. Again, nature and plant breeders have been prolific and there are numerous species and cultivars available. Many of the best of them are well proportioned for the restrictions of a small garden. And where a tall-growing tree is out of the question, two or three, identical or similar, can be clustered together with branches

accommodate *M. grandiflora.* Far hardier, it is a small, picturesque tree that grows to about 30 feet and carries purplish saucer-shaped flowers in spring. 'Alexandrina' has white on the inside of the petals, purple on the outside; 'Lennei' has dark purplish balloonlike flowers with white inside, but 'Lennei Alba' is pure white.

In fact, all magnolias make fine long-season ornamentals with their splendid flowers, attractive leaves, and good stance; they also have intrigu-ing knobby fruit, cucumber green at first, opening to reveal bright red seeds. Two other worthy magnolias among the battery of useful varieties are the sweet bay (*M. virginiana*) and the semishrub star magnolia (*M. stellata*), which is among the earliest to bloom—so early, in fact, that in my garden its blooms are sometimes nipped by frost. The sweet bay, which is semi-evergreen to evergreen in the South, has much to recommend it—lemon-scented creamy intertwined to shade or enclose a terrace or other sitting area.

For many of us, the flowering dogwood (*Cornus florida*) is unquestionably one of the most delightful flowering trees. It has a long and lovely flowering period; the flowers become bright red fruits, relished by birds; in autumn, its rich green leaves turn burgundy red or orange; and its distinct horizontal tiers of branches are appealing year in and year out. In the Northeast, the first dogwood to bloom is *C. mas,* known as cornelian cherry; this species puts out clusters of tiny yellow umbels on its bare branches when nothing else is blooming. Flowering dogwood comes into its own several weeks later, erupting near homes, in parks, and along the edges of woodlands in clouds of pink, rose, or white blossoms. (The "petals" are actually bracts that surround the tiny true flowers.) In recent years, *C. florida* has been beset by a fungal disease, which has decimated its numbers, but as the weaker trees have died off, the severity has lessened. New hybrids—the Stellar series—which are resistant to the common dogwood pests and diseases, are now available. The latest dogwood to flower is the kousa dogwood (*C. kousa*), a tidy, charming tree that displays its large white bracts face up on its branches; they hold up well on the tree and in water when cut.

The West Coast counterpart to the eastern flowering dogwood is mountain dogwood (*C. nuttallii,* z7–9), a larger tree with showy bracts—white flushed with pink.

There are smaller cultivars, some with attractive variegated leaves.

Some of the most beautiful spring-blossoming trees are the cherries, peaches, plums, and crab apples that have been bred for disease resistance and improved flowers rather than edible fruit. They are among the most popular choices for flowering ornamentals in the spring garden. Of the many flowering cherries, the Higan cherry (*Prunus subhirtella* var. *pendula*), with weeping branches clothed in single pink flowers, is one of the earliest to bloom. The Japanese, or Yoshino, cherry (*P. × yedoensis*) is famous for the display it puts on at the Tidal Basin in Washington, D.C., each year; its fragrant blossoms open light pink, then fade to white— a characteristic of many cherry trees. *P.* 'Hally Jolivette' is a dainty tree growing only to 12 feet, densely branched and rounded; its pink buds open to double white flowers, and a better flowering cherry tree for a small garden would be hard to find. (Its blossoms go so prettily with early flowering bulbs that one must resist the temptation to overplunder.)

Crab apple trees are the easiest of the flowering fruit trees to grow, provided a disease-resistant cultivar is chosen, and they are the most tolerant of winter cold. In fall, their branches dangle with bunches of red, orange, or yellow fruits to seduce the birds, put jelly on the pantry shelves, and decorate the house. One of my favorites is *Malus* 'Red Jade,' an enchanting little tree with glossy green leaves and slender arching branches,

BELOW *The blossoms of the ornamental crab apple* Malus 'Red Jade', *which assumes a graceful weeping form as it matures, overlaps with the bloom period of pearlbush* (Exochorda × macrantha), *framing the greenhouse.*

FACING PAGE *Flowering dogwood* (Cornus florida), *with its layered branches and lovely white petallike bracts, epitomizes spring in many parts of the country.*

ABOVE *In spring, pink or white blossoms cover the branches of ornamental fruit trees, such as the crab apples (*Malus *spp.) growing here in a range of sizes and forms at Rosedale Nurseries in Westchester County, New York. In fall, their yellow, orange, or red fruits are an added attraction, making them good candidates for the garden and for arrangements.*

BELOW *Azaleas (*Rhododendron *spp.) have bright, pretty flowers that range from pink, shown here, to golden yellow, apricot, and brilliant red.*

which begins its season with deep pink blossoms and ends it with ½-inch shining red fruits in fall. Another is the Japanese flowering crab apple, *M. floribunda,* for its plethora of pink-fading-to-white blooms, ⅜-inch yellow-red fruit, and distinctive winter silhouette of widely spreading branches.

Hawthorn trees belong to the same botanical family—Rosaceae— as the flowering fruit trees and are also desirable smallish ornamentals for home gardens. They bloom in spring or early summer with white, pink, or red blossoms and possess a good habit of growth and attractive showy fruits. They lend themselves as lawn specimens, hedges, and because of the efficient thorns on some, as barriers (but not near areas where children play). They include many native species, with their built-in hardiness. The Washington hawthorn (*Crataegus phaenopyrum*) is the best among them and will withstand urban rigors.

Most, but not all, deciduous trees

ABOVE *The buds of some crab apples are deep pink and open to pinkish or white blossoms—which may be double, or single as shown above. Branches may be cut early and forced into bloom indoors, or cut at various stages of flowering as desired.*

PAGES 46–47 *Flowering dogwood (*Cornus florida*), an old apple tree, sweet-scented* Viburnum carlesii, *and fragrant daphne in the foreground create a refreshing scene against spring green grass and foliage. A branch or two cut from each will re-create a similar mood indoors.*

flower in the spring. A few burst into bloom in summer, adding vertical color to the garden. The golden-rain tree (*Koelreuteria paniculata*) is one of the few yellow-flowering trees, touting clusters of flowers with orange blotches at the base of golden petals in summer. The Japanese snowbell (*Styrax japonicus*), a well-proportioned lawn or patio tree, blooms profusely in early summer with small, dangling white bells along the branches followed by gray berries in autumn. The Franklin tree (*Franklinia alatamaha*),

named for Benjamin Franklin and sometimes classified as a shrub, could pick up the slack in August, when its green leaves turn red and orange even as it opens its fragrant, camellialike flowers. These and others remind us again of the endless variety in nature, which challenges us to widen our own choices.

Scores of other deciduous (and evergreen) trees make fine candidates for the home landscape and for cutting. Among them are superb Japanese maples and cut-leaf cultivars,

birches, beeches, willows, catalpas, alders, chestnuts, laburnums, sourwood, sophoras, stewartias, Carolina silver-bell, lindens. . . . Trips to arboretums, botanical and public gardens, nurseries, and the surrounding countryside will provide living images to round out the information gathered from other sources. Because trees are generally intended to remain in place for a lifetime, they deserve extra consideration: choose them wisely, set them with care, and enjoy their timeless beauty.

Useful in the border or as a hedge, low-growing Spiraea × bumalda *'Anthony Waterer' covers itself with flat cerise flower clusters in June, blooms all summer, and will put out a second flush later if the flower heads are kept cut. The flowers and reddish green foliage, sometimes cream variegated, are both lovely in arrangements.*

SHRUBS

The armloads of flowering branches that lilacs, forsythias, mock oranges, viburnums, spireas, and rhododendrons provide early in the season are mainstays in many a spring bouquet. They are all valuable shrubs, the durable workhorses of many landscapes.

Shrubs go to work for us in various ways. Planted next to the house they can camouflage an unattractive foundation wall, soften architectural lines, frame a doorway, shield the house from glaring sun. They are commonly planted with trees to delineate property lines and as hedges to mark off different sections of the garden, to conceal unsightly garbage cans and views, and for privacy. They are unarguably the most versatile, utilitarian group of plants for the home garden.

Shrubs perform these services with great style and timing, even offering armloads of flowers before spring arrives; leaves in tender colors of spring green, primrose yellow, muted purple, red, and silver, changing tints as summer progresses; and fiery foliage, berries and seedpods for birds and vases in fall, and glistening twigs and shapes in winter. The array of flower shapes is staggering: voluptuous domes of hydrangeas and viburnums, arching wands of spirea and fountain buddleia (*Buddleia alternifolia*), fuzzy billows of smokebush, ruffly bowls of tree peonies. Leaf size and texture range from tiny, ferny tamarisk to glossy, veiny fingers of evergreen leucothoe, Oregon grape, pittosporum, and *Pieris japonica.* Foliage can have a glossy or mat finish, be of one color or variegated, come in every shade of green, or traverse the color wheel. These are all wonderful design elements for the flower arranger.

A judicious selection of shrubs can assure that your vases never go empty. A single substantial woody stem of witch hazel or flowering quince can add just the right odd grace note to a chinoiserie or milkglass vase to make a refreshing early spring display, and a harbinger of blossoms to come. For flowers alone, the season kicks off with winter honeysuckle (*Lonicera fragrantissima*), winter jasmine, witch hazel, and the goat willow (*Salix caprea*), a fine pussy willow for forcing indoors in water. A handful of choices from a thousand other shrubs can carry through to keep garden and house aglow all year. Every color of the spectrum is represented, sometimes all in one shrub as it matures through the season.

Because shrubs are intermediate plants, falling between trees and the more ephemeral herbaceous plants, they can be used compatibly with each group. Planted in front of trees, they serve as visual anchors. In a mixed border with other plants, shrubs add structure, heft, and variety of color, form, and texture. Perennials, annuals, and flowering bulbs can be interspersed in thoughtful combinations in the nooks and bays created by the shrubs. They lend themselves as supports for climbing plants—

clematis can easily climb up through and tumble over their branches—and ground covers can clothe their feet. The dividend from such high-rise arrangements, especially valuable in small gardens, is a plethora of pickings for bouquets.

Begin by making a list of sensible and attractive shrubs seen in other gardens, nurseries, or in books or bouquets. Then study up on their characteristics. Final decisions should hew to a few major axioms of good gardening to avoid possible regret later.

First, suit the plant to the place, not the other way around. This was a guiding manifesto of Charles Sprague Sargent, plant luminary and first director of the famous Arnold Arboretum in Boston. It is a good practice to buy your shrubs from local reputable nurseries, since presumably they will carry plants known to be hardy in your area and can offer advice on how and where to plant them in your garden. (Again, pay attention to microclimates in your garden.)

A shrub's light and soil needs must be met if it is to flourish and offer profuse blooms. Some shrubs prefer a sunny location, whereas others may tolerate or even require shade. Some prefer dry soil; others, wet. Some like a rich diet; others fare better when they are hungry. Be sure you can accommodate your selections.

Many shrubs do well in soils that are mildly acidic, slightly below 7.0 (neutral) on the pH scale. Ericaceous plants, such as rhododendrons and hollies, require a more acidic

soil, about pH 4.5–5. Have your soil tested through your county extension service; if necessary, the staff can suggest the proper amendments for adjusting the acid-alkaline ratio. Overly acidic soils can be sweetened by adding lime. If the pocket in your garden where you want to plant an acid-loving shrub is borderline alkaline, incorporating Canadian sphagnum moss into the soil may be sufficient to increase the acidity.

In gardening, as elsewhere, form follows function. Consider the job the shrub is to perform. Will it be part of a planting next to the house? Then size and shape are paramount. A low-growing, sweet-smelling daphne, or a three-foot-high Heavenly Blue bluebeard (*Caryopteris* × *clandonensis*) with misty, late-summer blossoms would be a better choice under a window than a *Buddleia davidii*, which can grow to eight feet and more in a single summer. Or choose the lovely The Bride pearlbush (*Exochorda* × *macrantha*), which will grow only to four feet, instead of the common pearlbush (*E. racemosa*), which can shoot past ten feet. Don't give up right away if a shrub you have set your heart on seems too tall for the location you have in mind; often a dwarf or low-growing form is available.

For certain other situations, a shrub with a contained or compact form would serve better than a gangly, spreading one. The thorny clutches of a firethorn (*Pyracantha* spp.) should not encroach into a doorway. Even if you do not mind

The whorled variegated leaves of Daphne × burkwoodii *'Carol Mackie' give it an attractive face even when it is not in bloom. In May when it is, this three-foot-tall shrub covers itself with small, light pink flowers in starry clusters. The flowers emit a powerful sweet fragrance that lasts in arrangements.*

the work of frequent pruning to keep shrubs in check (which should be unnecessary if you shop wisely), this often destroys their natural shape. It is better to avoid these drawbacks altogether than to rue them later.

If you want to block from view a work area or an ugly building, tall-growing evergreens with dense foliage make an effective year-round screen. Arborvitae, yew, and tall-growing boxwood are the classics; each is clippable, and all such foliage is useful to the arranger for rounding out bouquets. For a year-round wind-break of shrubs, try staggering an outer row of evergreens and an inner one of deciduous flowering shrubs, leaving ample space between to accommodate their breadth at maturity.

A loose natural screen for a terrace can be constructed by planting deciduous flowering shrubs that will allow breezes and sunlight to filter through; forsythia, azaleas (try the yellow-flowering *Rhododendron luteum*), viburnums (many good ones—but none more beautiful in bloom than Marie's double-file viburnum, *Viburnum plicatum* var. *tomentosum* 'Mariesii', which has to be seen to be believed), either spring- or summer-blooming spireas, clethra, and many others with open or ferny foliage can do the job.

Wild and cultivated shrubs that have naturalized make easy-care screens, but without pruning some may require more space than you can give them, so it is important to know

their mature size. A few possibilities are viburnums, bush honeysuckles, barberries, high-bush blueberries, winterberry (*Ilex verticillata*), and bayberry. Each can contribute something special for bouquets over the seasons.

For hedges, there is always privet. In warmer regions, evergreen varieties with lustrous leaves will grow rapidly—to 25 feet if not shorn back. (However, privets will become scraggly in a few years if left un-

trimmed.) In cooler climates, privets are either semievergreen or deciduous. Good choices for the Northeast are the pretty California privet (*Ligustrum ovalifolium*, z5–8) and the hardier Amur privet (*L. amurense*, z3–8). Golden-leaved varieties that fare well in dry conditions and near the seashore are distinctive both in the garden and in arrangements. Unpruned privet produces small white spring flowers (some object to their

odor) followed by black berries that are held on the plant into winter. The tiny-leaved bush honeysuckle *Lonicera nitida* and common boxwood (*Buxus sempervirens*) also make good hedges; like privet, they grow quickly and respond to frequent shearings by sprouting and sprouting again until a dense thicket forms.

With imagination, a number of other shrubs, both evergreen and deciduous, can be called into service as hedges. You can plant a single kind or,

A Virginia garden reflects an eclectic design with an Italianate flavor. A serene all-green allée of tall boxwood hedges, overhanging branches, and hostas line a raked dirt path leading to a wall fountain.

for a more informal effect, intersperse different species. Nothing provides a more flattering background to the flowers in a border than the soft, dark green needles of a yew hedge. Shear it or subject it to benign neglect. For a natural-looking hedge that requires little pruning, choose evergreen hollies with rich green leaves.

Rhododendrons are the most impressive evergreen flowering shrubs in much of the coastal Northwest, where conditions suit them perfectly,

A "personage," draped in ivy, appears among the pink-blushed buds and flowering trusses of Rhododendron *'Cunningham's White'. Landscape architect Betty Ajay has integrated the garden owners' passion for statuary into the planting, resulting in a garden full of surprises.*

and in parts of the Northeast. Their counterparts in the South are the stunning evergreen azaleas, which belong to the genus *Rhododendron* and have similar flowers. There are many different azaleas, both evergreen and deciduous, with flowers in an immense variety of colors, and bushes of different sizes and shapes. Many gardeners take pride in collecting these shrubs and feature them both as specimen plants and in groups in the landscape. Flowers of

the deciduous Exbury and Knap Hill azaleas embrace enchanting shades in the yellow-salmon-orange range. The pinxterbloom (*R. periclymenoides*), pink-shell azalea (*R. vaseyi*), and the delicate royal azalea (*R. schlippenbachii*, with translucent pink trusses) are breathtaking focal points in gardens in my area. The low-growing North Tisbury hybrids introduced by Polly Hill of Martha's Vineyard, Massachusetts, are ideal for small gardens.

There are too many others to list them here.

As for the members of the genus *Rhododendron* that we call rhododendrons, they reliably envelop themselves every spring in huge, airy globes of flowers, bringing drama to the garden. They are also valuable to the arranger, but their large trusses are so imposing in a vase that they are best kept to themselves with some of their foliage removed to reveal their faces. In the garden, they will flourish in good light under tall trees in acidic soil. As is true of azaleas, thousands of rhododendron cultivars exist. The critical factor in picking varieties for your garden is their winter-hardiness, which differs remarkably from cultivar to cultivar. Again, it is wise to buy them from local nurseries, and see them in bloom to assure the color you want. Blossoms come in white, yellow, pink, rose, lavender, or purple, often with central splotches of another shade or hue. There are dwarf and tall varieties, as well as small-leaved and large-leaved kinds. Rhododendrons look best grouped with their own kind, or with other acid-loving plants such as Japanese pieris, camellias, hollies, enkianthus, and skimmia. For optimum bloom, remove spent flower heads each year before their energy is invested in setting seed. Aside from their dramatic flowers and year-round value in the garden, you will have a source of handsome, glossy foliage to mix in winter bouquets with a few purchased flowers—fragrant rubrum lilies perhaps. The bold foliage,

A raised shrubbery in Oregon, packed with mophead and lacecap hydrangeas (Hydrangea macrophylla) and deciduous azaleas, and edged with blue violas and lobelia, offers a long season of bloom. The hydrangeas, grown from cuttings taken years ago, offer armloads of blooms for arranging.

often covered underneath in brown felt, is reusable for several arrangements, stands well by itself for an all-green display, and can be preserved in glycerin.

I prefer my rhododendrons clothed with either white or pink flowers. Scintillation is a luminous pink, grows to eight feet, and is widely available. Trude Webster is a five-foot pink-flowering competitor from the Northwest. Boule de Neige is a classic white; Dora Amateis is a compact white hybrid. The Yakushimanum hybrids are also wonderful compact plants, growing to about four feet and desirable for small gardens.

The small-leaved, early-flowering P.J.M. is another space saver, growing to just under six feet in my garden. In late April, my three shrubs, planted against a gray rock outcropping, cheer the cold landscape by erupting in clouds of deep lavender-pink blossoms that completely hide their branches (provided they escape browsing deer). Just a branch or two in a vase adds warmth to a white-walled room. In late fall, the leaves turn to burgundy; brought indoors in winter they prove a mar-velous foil for needled branches. (Local chapters of The American Rhododendron Society welcome requests for information on cultivars and growing practices.)

Officially roses, too, are shrubs. No flowers are more universally loved and praised for their elegant forms, velvety textures, limitless range of melting and torrid colors, and delicate fragrances. They have a long and rich history, encrusted with legend and poetry. Roses can be found growing in gardens throughout the world. It would be folly to attempt to do justice to this large genus of beloved plants about which countless books have been written, but it's worth mentioning a few of the species roses that can be remarkably gratifying as landscape shrubs.

Unlike modern hybrid tea roses (which admittedly are durable in bouquets), species roses will not sulk if you fail to pamper them, and are so hardy that they will hold their own with other shrubs. One among them, Father Hugo's rose (*Rosa xanthina* f. *hugonis*), is the first to bloom in my garden in earliest spring. It has the unadulterated charm of all wild roses, with long, arching stems and rich yellow single flowers. The leaves are discreet and dainty, until fall when they turn reddish orange. The sprays are as captivating in a pewter mug as they are bending toward the gray boulder the shrub adorns in the garden. It has one flaw (maybe two, as the roses shatter quickly when cut), which I willingly forgive: it has no scent. Perhaps a wiser choice for a yellow rose would be fragrant, semidouble Harison's Yellow. But my rose was given me years ago by a wonderful Scotsman, my gardening mentor, now gone. It was the first rosebush I planted, and in the same spirit with which it was given to me, its heirs now grow in the gardens of friends.

I also find the Kiftsgate rose (*R. filipes* 'Kiftsgate'), a climber, useful for spontaneous bouquets. It is so eager to please that I sometimes feel it could fill all the vases of the world in June with its small, sweetly fragrant white roses and still not ex-

haust itself. It is planted against a post-and-rail fence, and in its third summer it spanned the entire length of 60 feet. This rose is difficult to find, but worth the search. A clematis, *Clematis* 'Comtesse de Bouchard', shares the same planting hole, picking up the color slack, while the Kiftsgate rests, with pink-mauve blooms pinned to creamy stamens.

Among the best roses for informal flowering shrubs are the rugged rugosa roses (*R. rugosa*), which are disease-free and will grow in poor soil. The semidouble Blanc Double de Coubert is my first choice among the whites; among the pinks, Frau Dagmar Hastrup for its satiny petals and respectable foliage. Both have a delicious fragrance. The rugosas make an almost impenetrable hedge if sheared back every other year or so (I cut mine down to about two feet in April). The blooms are nice for throwing together a last-minute centerpiece, but they collapse quickly. The hips are most useful for jelly or tea, for fall arrangements, and for the birds.

On the whole, shrubs are vigorous and self-reliant, and many will withstand years of neglect. However, even a little careful pruning will improve a shrub's health and prevent it from acquiring the slovenly, rangy look that often results from neglect. Prune to enhance its natural shape—shortening straggly growths and thinning out entire branches here and there. Save the crewcuts for shrubs in formal plantings.

Pruning determines a plant's shape

and influences how many flowers and leaves it will put out. Some hedges need to be clipped regularly for dense growth and good shape, especially privet. Conifers seldom need pruning except for light shaping, which can be done when cutting branches for a basket of winter greenery; otherwise, prune lightly in spring. Flowering shrubs with small, twiggy branches such as beauty bush, flowering quince, witch hazel, corylopsis, cotoneasters, and daphnes also require little pruning. Tree peonies, the most aristocratic shrubs of all, need only to have weak or dead wood removed. Lilacs, deutzia, and weigela maintain their vitality if some of the older branches are cut to the ground every year or so.

Any good book on shrubs or gardening techniques will tell you how and when to prune specific evergreen and deciduous shrubs and hedges. But understanding the underlying logic will help guide your pruning shears.

Pruning, in general, forces new growth and multiple branching and eventually more flowers; some conifers are a major exception. The time to prune depends on when buds form on a shrub, so some familiarity with your plant's biological time clock is necessary. In general, prune shrubs as soon after flowering as practical: spring bloomers in early summer, summer bloomers in winter or early spring. Use long-handled loppers and sharp scissorlike pruning shears, rather than the anvil types, which can crush stems.

BELOW *The lovely gallica shrub rose Empress Josephine blooms in the author's garden with the vigorous climbing species rose Rosa filipes 'Kiftsgate', with fragrant, creamy white flowers and yellow stamens. Roses are a law unto themselves when it comes to pruning, and a good handbook should be consulted for directions. The Kiftsgate rose, which will bloom in shade and often is seen climbing into trees, rarely requires pruning except to check it. The blossoms make a lovely bouquet by themselves or when used as a filler with other flowers.*

FACING PAGE *A rose garden high on a bluff overlooking the Atlantic on the North Shore of Massachusetts holds antique and modern roses that can hold their own against an east wind and, at times, relentless sun. The climber on the arch is Dortmund, a single red with a white eye, vigorous and hardy. A few of the many old roses that grow well here are Maiden's Blush, Fantin-Latour, Rosa Mundi, Tuscany, and Empress Josephine. Among the modern roses are Queen Elizabeth, Golden Girl, and Buff Beauty.*

Summer-flowering shrubs that bloom on the current season's growth, such as buddleias, Rose-of-Sharon, and crepe myrtles, can be pruned in early spring before new growth starts. A greater number of shrubs bloom in spring or early summer—many lilacs, azaleas, spireas, viburnums, and myriads of others. They blossom from buds formed on the previous summer's growth. If you were to prune these shrubs in early spring, you would be cutting off flower buds scheduled to bloom that season. The time to prune these shrubs is soon after they stop flowering, before new growth begins.

Cut branches for the house with an eye toward improving the shape of the shrub; in effect, you will be accomplishing your pruning at the same time. Leave some of the flowers on the shrub if you want berries to develop. The cut branches can be edited further as you arrange them. Discreet pruning will leave something attractive to look at in the garden as well as in the house, and allows the shrub to replenish itself in the coming season.

THE CUTTING GARDEN

Bulbs

Annuals

I grow flowers to gather them, both for the house and to give away. We keep about sixty vases full in the house from late May until October, and never allow more than two colours in the same room. I have a yellow room where only yellow and white flowers, or white and blue, are permitted. A pink room for white and pink or pink and crimson; and a hall whose dominant tone is a rich red, where the flowers are red and white.

—Helena Rutherfurd Ely

A Woman's Hardy Garden, *1903*

ABOVE *Canterbury bells* (Campanula medium)*, a biennial, will last ten days or more as a cut flower if its stem ends are seared before conditioning. Different varieties will bloom from June to September.*

FACING PAGE *Flowers from the cutting garden at Monticello, in Virginia, provide arrangements for the house museum. Picking buckets contain nicotiana, delphinium, butterfly weed, zinnia, scabiosa, globe thistle, artemisia, yarrow, and various daisies.*

PAGES 56–57 *The bold leaves of zucchini separate snapdragons and gladioluses in a Virginia cutting garden. Gladioluses may be left in the ground year-round in the south, but the corms must be lifted and reset annually north of Zone 7.*

PAGE 57 *White lace flower* (Ammi majus)*, an annual, has flowers that are similar to those of Queen-Anne's-lace and bloom in time for June wedding arrangements.*

The heyday of cutting gardens spanned the period from the late 1800s until the 1940s, coinciding with the golden era of country places in garden history. It was a time when banking and industrial barons built splendiferous estates on hundreds of thousands of acres across the country. In the showcase gardens surrounding their mansions, they created boxwood mazes, tree-lined allées, moated Temples of Love, Italianate fountains, and other features of the European gardens they admired. These extravagant paradises became the setting for opulent social events that fueled the society columns of the day.

Ornamental horticulture was taken seriously, and the new plants imported from abroad to be grown in the gardens often found their way into the trade. The owners lived their town-and-country lives surrounded by flowers indoors and out, grown in enormous cutting gardens and in spacious glasshouses, vying with each other for first-place awards in elaborate flower shows held in New York, Philadelphia, and other cities. To plant the vegetables, tend the gar-

dens, and keep the croquet lawns rolled, they employed staffs of as many as 50 or more gardeners. The Depression first curtailed activities on these labor-intensive estates, and when World War II began, many of the workers went off to dig trenches instead of gardens. This drying-up of the cheap labor pool, added to rising taxes and the changing economic and social climate that followed the war, led to the demise of the country place. (*The Golden Age of American Gardens,* by Mac Griswold and Eleanor Weller, chronicles this fascinating period of garden history.)

At the other end of this spectrum were those flower lovers who have since time immemorial tucked extra plants for picking into makeshift cutting gardens—in vegetable and herb gardens, in nooks and crannies in the backyard. Today's cutting garden is an extension and a refinement of this hallowed practice of setting aside space in the garden where plants are grown solely for cutting to decorate the rooms of the house.

The unique benefit a separate cutting garden offers is freedom to grow what pleases you for bouquets

without concern for garden design; to cut every Peppermint Stick zinnia, every Madame Butterfly snapdragon, and every Sensation cosmos for bouquets if that is your heart's desire. Indeed, the point of having a separate cutting garden is to keep the more decorative parts of your property intact. This is a sane and positive concern, and a practice that gardeners over the years and across the ocean have respected. In *Flower Decoration in the House* (1903), Gertrude Jekyll speaks in an approving voice of "that part of the reserve garden in which flowers may be cut to any extent without robbing the more important and well-dressed portions of the pleasure grounds."

Besides this obvious advantage, a cutting garden hidden away from public eyes offers the gardener a place for unfettering the soul. All those repressed desires for sassy or brassy plants, the ones deemed in some circles to be banal or tasteless, can be expressed. In it you can dare to try a few voluptuous dahlias, dwarf gladioluses, hot-colored geraniums, and other flower border outcasts, which might add just the pizzazz a bouquet occasionally needs.

The notion that a separate cutting garden must be large to be productive and that it is labor-intensive persists in the minds of many flower lovers who are gardeners, cheating them of their due. The appropriate size for such a garden actually is simply one you can manage and your garden can accommodate. Whether it will yield handfuls or armloads of

flowers will depend to a large extent on its dimensions, a case where bigger is indeed better. But even a space as small as ten feet by five feet planted with annuals and a few well-chosen long-blooming perennials can yield a surprising number of blossoms. Select from heavy-flowering annuals such as spiky *Salvia farinacea* 'Blue Bedder', larkspur, zinnias, cosmos, snapdragons, tall marigolds in primrose yellow or creamy white, and *Ageratum* 'Blue Horizon', which has long stems, and plant an edging of the nasturtium *Tropaeolum majus* 'Alaska', which has variegated foliage. Perennials such as yarrow and the daisylike golden marguerite, shasta daisy, feverfew, or purple-pink coneflower will give you nice round forms for bouquets; blue, pink, or white veronica or liatris will provide vertical accents. For efficient use of space, a second string of annuals could be started in flats for transplanting to the cutting garden to replace the first batch when flowering begins

to slacken. Foliage from ivy, ferns, hostas, and herbs (mint, lavender, sage), poached from other parts of your garden, can provide greenery and diversity of texture.

You might also want to tuck in a few plants that are easy to dry for winter bouquets, such as globe amaranth, strawflowers, statice, or cockscomb, and a few annual grasses such as ornamental wheat that mix so well with the everlastings. With contributions from other parts of the garden, which can be picked over lightly, your cutting garden will make a world of difference in how often you can have bouquets to cheer house and heart. After the garden has been planted and mulched, it will be relatively care-free. Your main job will be the pleasant one of keeping the flowers cut, not only for bouquets but to encourage the plants to put their energies into producing more flowers, not seeds.

The crux of the matter is location. A cutting garden is primarily a

LEFT *This cutting garden in Lake Forest, Illinois, is conveniently sited next to the greenhouse. While not totally concealing the area, a hedge and grape arbor separate it attractively from the garden proper.*

FACING PAGE, TOP *The owner of this backyard garden in Evanston, Illinois, an avid arranger of dried flowers, grows his own mainstays for drying. Shown here in one of several beds is feverfew, the bee balm* Monarda didyma *'Cambridge Scarlet', purple coneflower,* Lythrum *'Morden's Pink', snapdragons, white and blue larkspur, and the mealy-cup sage* Salvia farinacea *'Victoria'.*

FACING PAGE, BOTTOM *Rudbeckia, phlox, and loosestrife grow in this well-groomed cutting garden along with other long-blooming perennials and a few vegetables—tomatoes, lettuce and rhubarb.*

ABOVE *The author's cutting garden holds a changing array of plants for bouquets and for experimenting. Annuals such as zinnias, marigolds, nicotiana, cosmos, and hollyhocks grow mainly on the left, perennials started from seed on the right, and chives, comfrey, and self-sown dill around the pump.*

FACING PAGE *In early summer, poppies, delphiniums, and clematis bloom among cabbages (under the mesh tunnel), chives, and rhubarb in a flower lover's kitchen garden in Massachusetts.*

flower factory, so for maximum production the requisites are the same as for any flower bed: good soil with adequate drainage and a minimum of six hours of full sun a day. Less sun won't preclude having flowers for cutting, but it will limit your options to growing only shade-tolerant plants.

Historically, cutting gardens have been hidden away in a place that cannot be seen from the front of the house, sitting terrace, or living room or dining room picture window. There is good reason for maintaining this tradition. If the cutting garden is constantly in view, it becomes an integral part of the decorative landscape. One may then have to think twice about cutting from it, perhaps defeating its purpose.

Assess every possibility: wasted space in a corner behind the garage, near the back doorway, in a bay created by shrub plantings, at the rear of your property, around a bend in the garden currently given over to lawn. It should also be near a water source. Fabricate a hiding place if none exists, perhaps by secluding the cutting garden behind a hedge of yew, privet, bush honeysuckle, or other fast-growing shrubs. (The same effect can be achieved in much less time by planting a curtain of vines around a fence; clematis, perennial sweet pea, morning-glory, and cup-and-saucer vine (*Cobaea scandens*) are all good choices, and all, except for morning-glories, make good cut flowers.)

The main goal in preparing the garden and laying it out is to provide a healthy environment for the plants that will grow there. If the land is raw and weedy, it should be cleared, dug at least to the depth of the spade, and the soil amended with organic matter. This might be compost, ripened manure, or leaf mold, each of which would improve the tilth of the soil and offer a modest boost of fertilizer.

How you go about clearing weeds, adding nutrients to soil, and subsequently mulching and spraying will depend on your philosophy about the environment in general. Some gardeners focus on good cultural practices using biological controls and insecticides derived from natural sources such as poisonous plants. These must be used with care, but they degrade quickly in the environment. Others choose chemical sprays and products that will do the least harm to the environment and use them carefully. More earth- and people-friendly products are now available as alternatives to petroleum-based chemicals—some of which are harmful—providing more responsible options to gardeners.

Traditionally, cutting gardens are planted like vegetable gardens, straight rows running north and south, with about 18 inches between rows. This gives each plant its fair share of light and a fighting chance for maximum air circulation, water, and nutrients. I find that three feet is a good width for the main path, allowing wheelbarrow or garden-cart

clearance and turnaround; two feet is ample for secondary paths. You may prefer to divide the plot into smaller rectangular blocks, less than four or five feet wide, so you can reach into the flower beds from both sides without stepping in them. You may lay out the garden by flower color, giving over each block or row to flowers of one color.

This straightforward layout is geared for efficiency. However, making the cutting garden an inviting workplace for the gardener can also induce productivity. Bring in a birdbath, or a bench or seat (even a hefty log turned on end) for roosting and gathering strength to yank out the next passel of weeds, should you have neglected to mulch between the rows of young plants.

Grass paths in a cutting garden are impractical. Instead, pave the main path with rounds of wood or fieldstones and plant creeping thyme between them. A good dose of wood chips or pea gravel (not white, which

BELOW *To keep the soil moist and eliminate weeding, rows between cosmos, zinnias, and white lace flower (Ammi majus) in this production garden are mulched with several inches of straw placed on top of layers of newspaper.*

FACING PAGE, TOP *In September, dahlias take over a corner of the author's second cutting garden, hidden in a work area next to a compost pile and raspberry patch. Earlier, it supplies blooms of peonies, irises, and lilies to augment border pickings for the house.*

FACING PAGE, BOTTOM *In early June, the border of Pauline Runkle, a floral designer in Manchester, Massachusetts, provides a variety of shapes, textures, and colors for arranging—roses, lady's-mantle, astilbes, campanulas, dianthus, columbines, foxgloves, yarrow, and poppies—some just beginning to bloom.*

PAGES 66–67 *Annual cosmos, bachelor's-buttons, poppies, and marigolds are thickly planted for picking in terraced beds on an estate in Virginia.*

is too glaring in sun) rolled along main paths will give an even foothold, keep weeds down, and keep feet dry. An edging of some sort—railroad ties, bricks, or stones on end—will keep loose materials out of the planting beds.

A resourceful gardener in my area gets fantastic results from her novel mulching method. First, she spreads thick layers of the *New York Times* on the soil between the rows of plants. On top of these, she lavishly strews bedding straw hauled from the barn of a neighbor who raises llamas. This exotic blanket keeps down weeds and eventually decomposes, enriching the soil as it does. For the rest of us, run-of-the-mill materials such as plain marsh or salt hay, which is weed-free, fluffed out to a depth of five inches or so over any black-and-white newspapers will do an admirable job.

Because annuals bloom so profusely and so tirelessly, some from June until frost, they hold pride of place in the cutting garden. If in addition it can accommodate a few spring bulbs or perennials, these will enrich your arrangements, but choose carefully. Don't grow tons of flowers you don't need and won't have time to cut. It's easy to go overboard, and waste time and money in the process.

Perennials take up more room per plant than most annuals, an average of three square feet per mature plant. For that kind of luxury in a cutting garden, a plant should pay by blooming floriferously and over a long period, which is asking a lot of a perennial, which must harbor its energy to come back and bloom again the next year, and the next. Some of the most beloved classics—Oriental poppies, peonies, irises, some delphiniums—bloom fleetingly for two weeks or so and then take a back seat for the rest of the season. From a practical standpoint, these rarely justify the space they would take up in a small cutting garden, but some gardeners may not mind the sacrifice for their wonderful blooms. Chances are that a place in the sun outside of the cutting garden could be found to accommodate these old favorites, perhaps clumped in front of shrubs growing at the perimeter of your property. The solid shapes and substantial foliage of most shrubs will help camouflage gaps resulting from cutting the flowers in front.

Bulbs

It is exhilarating to go out in early spring after the long gray winter to find the garden painted in fresh swatches of color by small flowering bulbs—snowdrops, crocuses, scillas, and others—soon to be followed by daffodils and tulips. "I always think that this, the time of Tulips, is the season of all the year when the actual arranging of flowers affords the greatest pleasure," Gertrude Jekyll observed in *Flower Decoration in the House.* "The rush and heat of summer have not yet come; the days are still fairly restful, and one is so glad to greet and handle these early blossoms."

No garden should be without daffodils, from the classic golden King Alfred and Unsurpassable to the newer kinds. Rather than grow them in the cutting garden, try to establish a planting elsewhere on your lot, if you haven't already done so, and allow them to naturalize. Daffodils (which belong to the genus *Narcissus* and are sometimes called narcissus) are disdained by and poisonous to many animals; unlike tulips, they grow unmolested by deer, gophers, woodchucks, raccoons, squirrels, and rabbits. Because they spread by multiplying, a few years' time will produce a scene of Wordsworthian splendor from which you can cut abundant blooms without making a noticeable dent. Failing that, daffodils relegated to a corner in the cutting garden would not be too greedy of space. Try some of the novelty ones that come in bicolor shades of salmon, orange, red, and rose.

All daffodil hybrids are worthy, depending on what appeals: big trumpets, big cups or small cups, flat faces, recurved petals, bunch-flowered, and so on. Some are intensely fragrant. Do include the poet's narcissus (*Narcissus poeticus*), with its quaint open face centered with a small yellow "eye." The variety with a red-rimmed eye is known as pheasant's eye narcissus (*N. poeticus* var. *recurvus*). A handful cut will scent a whole room.

All tulips are enchanting and deserve space in the cutting garden. They are exquisite in arrangements, either bunched by themselves in glass containers that show their handsome stems or mixed with other flowers. The stems trace graceful lines when allowed to bend and curve; the flowers are intriguing to watch as they turn toward the light, open their petals to disclose exquisite dark markings, then close into cups, globes, and almond shapes. Tulip flowers finish their life cycle with great dignity—often blooms will plop their petals all at once to get it over with as neatly as possible.

Early-blooming tulips include species and Greigii and Kaufmanniana hybrids; midseason ones, Darwin hybrids and peony-flowered forms; and various late-bloomers. You can select them so that you will have tulips from April to June in your choice of color, form, and size, with single or double petals. Many tulip flowers will last three weeks in the garden or five to seven days in water. The midseason Darwin hybrids (a

tulips. Fringed, twisted petals with green markings and arching stems evoke an exotic playfulness in bouquets. Glossy maroon-black Black Parrot is especially fanciful. Combine it with pristine, white single tulips for drama in a vase. For more intrigue, throw in a baker's dozen of the streaked Rembrandts with their fantastic "broken" color patterns (ironically caused by a virus), which set off a craze for tulips in Holland in the seventeenth century.

After daffodils and tulips have finished blooming, their foliage must be allowed to grow, and eventually turn yellow, while the underground bulb stores up food for the next bloom season. In the cutting garden, unlike the display border, you can simply ignore the unsightly foliage and allow nature to take its course. If you want to make better use of the space, grow shallow-rooted annuals between the bulbs. Either start plants of ageratum, snapdragons, or zinnias on the side or in the cold frame and

ABOVE Darwin tulips, with their pure form, clear colors, and strong stems, are superior for cutting, but double forms in soft, somber, and brilliant hues are also exceptionally lovely. Select large, firm bulbs for the best bloom, and plant at least half a dozen of a given variety to make a splash on the landscape; a cutting garden is the perfect place for growing extras and odds and ends.

RIGHT Tulips are grown by the hundreds each year in this cutting garden in Greenwich, Connecticut, where they must be protected from hungry deer. The colors are restricted to the orange-coral tones that work well inside the house, and the flowers are selected to bloom from mid-April to mid-May, when the owners are in residence. The bulbs are then lifted and placed in the shade to cure, after which annuals and vegetables take over the cutting beds. The tulip bulbs are replanted in the fall.

cross between the later-blooming Darwins and Fosteriana tulips) capture the purity and simplicity that are the essence of tulips and are always desirable. The blowsy peony-flowered tulips are lovely and long lasting in water, if you can keep them from being ruined by spring winds and rain.

While there is no unworthy tulip, it is the later-flowering tulips that are most irresistible. The cottage tulips are easier to handle in arrangements than the stiffer, more formal Darwins. The popular lily-flowered tulips are similar to the cottage ones but have long, pointed, recurving petals. I first saw White Triumphator, one of the best, in Rosemary Verey's garden in the English Cotswolds several years ago. Its satiny petals glistening against intermingled blue forget-me-nots reinforced that "careless rapture" that characterizes her garden and captivates all who visit it.

Parrot tulips are sports of other

transplant them in spots between the tulips as they go dormant, or scatter seeds of the hardy annual love-in-a-mist (*Nigella damascena*) on the ground between bulbs in early spring; by the time the tulips stop flowering, the fast-growing seedlings will hide the unattractive foliage and supply a new crop of flowers. Some gardeners dig up their tulips with the foliage intact and allow them to ripen in a shaded spot with good air circulation; the bulbs are then stored and replanted in the fall. My tulip bulbs usually become exhausted in a few years and I replace them with new varieties. (For more on spring bulbs, see page 169 in the Plant Profiles section.)

Annuals

Annuals complete their life cycle in one season, then perish. Their brief life-span is climaxed by blooming furiously, then setting seed to assure the survival of the species. By removing their flowers before seed is set, either by cutting or deadheading, the plants are stimulated to put out more flowers.

There are hundreds of species of annuals, and thousands of varieties. They come in all sizes, forms, textures, and especially colors. Gardening with annuals is very much a matter of gardening with color, for this is their most impressive quality. Hybridizers have bred annual flowers in every shade and tint imaginable, which can be found by searching seed and nursery catalogs. Being venturous and trying new annuals each year will give you a

chance to discover which colors and color combinations enhance your indoor decor. (See pages 94–100 for a discussion of color.)

Selecting annual flowers from the overwhelming number available can be daunting. Above all, choose plants that will grow in the conditions your garden offers. Annuals in general are extremely adaptable to a wide range of growing conditions, but some have special needs: hot or cool summers, sandy or peaty soil, watering in times of drought (an important consideration in parts of the country with little rainfall). Begin by checking cultural information given in seed and nursery catalogs and go from there; also see the Bibliography.

Judge how annuals will look not in the cutting garden but up close in a vase. Relatively long, strong stems and long-lasting flowers when cut are pluses. Most annuals will last a week in water; China asters, coreopsis, marigolds, zinnias, and others may last as long as two weeks.

Gaily colored streaked and blended tulips, grown in the cutting garden shown on the facing page, pick up the colors and circus mood of the Italian pottery pitcher and mugs.

Look for variety in flower form, size, and texture, with a mix of spiky, rounded, and airy "filler" shapes for well-balanced bouquets. Good foliage is nice but not essential, as leaves can be stripped from the stems and other foliage substituted. Include some flowers for the fragrance they will bring to a room, such as heliotrope, petunias, stocks, and some nicotiana.

Recently, plant lovers have been rediscovering the merits of antique annuals, cultivated species over a hundred years old; these are plants that have been left untouched by plant hybridizers, and many gardeners prefer their classic form to the bigger blobs of color and blurred flower shapes that characterize some

of the annual hybrids. Seed companies now offer antique varieties of selected annuals—zinnias, marigolds, cosmos, nasturtiums, larkspur, sweet peas, and others—along with the latest hybrids.

As for zinnias, a mainstay of summer bouquets, any palette can be satisfied. For example, you could choose the old-fashioned Chippendale, which could have been the inspiration behind Katharine S. White's engaging description of zinnias in *Onward and Upward in the Garden:* "a nice flower . . . clean-cut, of interesting, positive form, with formal petals that are so neatly and cunningly put together, and with colors so subtle yet clear, that they have always been the delight of the still-life

ABOVE *Individual beds stuffed with zinnias, yarrow, and red crocosmias evoke a Victorian style of planting that brightens this Virginia garden. The tight planting and ebullient flowering offer blooms which can be freely cut without spoiling the overall effect.*

FACING PAGE *Marigolds (*Tagetes *spp.) are rewarding, easy-to-grow plants, producing immense quantities of flowers in shades of sunny yellow and orange, as shown here, as well as cream and white. Some varieties have a fresh pungent smell, which some find unpleasant, but others have no scent.*

artist." Pink Ruffles, cactus-flowered with ruffled petals, is another lovely choice, as is the dahlia-type Border Beauty in mixed colors, including salmon, or Envy with its witty green blooms. Most zinnias are prone to mildew. The Border Beauty and Pulcino Mix series and Rose Pinwheel are mildew-resistant.

Many a bouquet would be enhanced by the vertical form and fluffy spires of snapdragons; I grow both the Rocket and Madame Butterfly

van Gogh's haunting paintings; pick four-inch flowers on four-foot plants of Lemon Queen if you consider yellow to be the essential color; otherwise, Velvet Queen, with velvety red flowers with dark centers, and elegant Italian White, sporting a gold zone and black center, will add zing to your floral still lifes.

Nicotiana, or flowering tobacco, an easy annual, is useful for its nodding form, which softens flowers such as scabiosa. The greenish-yellow

ABOVE *California poppy* (Eschscholzia californica) *has finely cut silver-green foliage that vies with its silky cups in attractiveness. The blooms on some varieties may close in late afternoon, but they are beautiful even when "asleep." Properly conditioned, they will last in arrangements for several days.*

MIDDLE *Blue and white spikes of mealy-cup sage* (Salvia farinacea), *a staple in many cutting gardens and borders, are entwined here with pink petunias.*

RIGHT *Pink and purple bracts of* Salvia viridis, *another annual sage, are long blooming and good for cutting and for drying.*

series. In soft, ambiguous colors—florets in salmon, peach, or apricot tints with muted sulfur or golden throats—they are sublime with a few blooms of lemon yellow coreopsis, creamy zinnias, and blue hydrangeas. Also indispensable are the blue spiky blooms of *Salvia farinacea* 'Blue Bedder', which is taller than *S. f.* 'Victoria' and is also better for drying.

Hand-sized flowers of annual sunflowers (*Helianthus annuus*) make dramatic bouquets reminiscent of

sprays of *Nicotiana langsdorffii* or the lime-sherbet flowers of *N. alata* 'Lime Green' are striking in a mixed bouquet with blue cornflowers or blue China asters and white baby's-breath.

Love-in-a-mist features intriguing round, puffy seedpods as winsome as its blue, pink, or white flowers. The variety named Miss Jekyll (which she herself proclaimed "the best garden nigella") has semidouble flowers in white, rose, or blue; the flowers, borne on 18-inch stems,

seem to float like starry balls of colored air amid its finely cut leaves. (If you wish seedpods for dried arrangements, you must leave some blooms uncut so seeds may form.)

Try love-lies-bleeding (*Amaranthus caudatus*) at least once. This unwieldy plant might not suit your flower border, but could be given a corner of the cutting garden. Its bizarre flowers set the Victorians back on their heels, and these long-lasting tassled red ropes still make a good conversa-

tion piece when placed in a tall vase. (Milton crowned the angels in *Paradise Lost* with flowers of amaranthus.) The Mexican sunflower (*Tithonia rotundifolia*) is a Jack-in-the-beanstalk kind of plant that would look silly in a small border but will proudly rise to eight feet in a season if given a corner of the cutting garden. It uses its space economically as a vertical warehouse for the dozens of sunny, orange-faced daisies it flaunts well into fall, nice complements for

ABOVE *Flats of annuals, ready for transplanting, are laid out like a quilt at Sassafras Nursery in California. Many gardeners start some annuals from seed and purchase seedlings of others from nurseries as a practical way to furnish the garden.*

MIDDLE *Large sunflowers (Helianthus spp.) with blooms perhaps eight inches across are good for bold arrangements. The double-flowered varieties with overlapping petals are more interesting than the single forms. Miniature sunflowers with daisylike flower heads measuring three inches across are good mixers with other flowers.*

LEFT *Spider flower (Cleome hasslerana), a prolific self-seeding annual, provides wispy blooms in white and shades of pink for airy bouquets.*

Colorful squares of pelargoniums, petunias, zinnias, marigolds, snapdragons, salvias, and impatiens grow in field trials at Goldsmith Seeds' research station in Gilroy, California. The new varieties and hybrids that are developed each year reach the home gardener in seed packets or as market packs of seedlings from growers.

autumn leaves and sapphire-berried *Symplocos paniculata.*

Most garden centers and nurseries carry seedlings of the most popular and common annuals. To get the most from the cutting garden, however, and to grow the varieties you want, you will need to grow at least some of them from seed. Annuals are generally easy to start and, unlike most perennials, give almost immediate and inexpensive gratification. Moreover, you will be participating in a time-honored ritual

that will tune you in to the unfolding of a plant's life cycle.

Propagating from seed is the best way to be sure of having the right flowers for a special event. For a summer wedding, seedlings begun indoors of the white lace flower (*Ammi majus*) can be set out in rows in the cutting garden after the last frost (sow the seeds in individual peat pots for easy transplanting). The flowers resemble the later-blooming Queen-Anne's-lace and make ravishing bouquets with delphiniums, Asiatic lilies, and roses collected from other parts of the garden. For a Fourth-of-July family reunion, a bouquet of shasta daisies, blue *Salvia farinacea*, red dianthus or snapdragons, and a few gray-white leaves of dusty miller stuck in a beanpot on the picnic table is an easy patriotic assemblage.

Seeds for many desirable annuals may be sown in the garden after the last spring frost. Sow the seeds of some, such as California poppies and zinnias, at two-week intervals until about mid-June to provide a steady supply for cutting throughout the season. Some of the seed companies offer packets of annual seed mixes prepared especially for the cutting garden. If you are new to gardening, try sowing a packet of these easy-to-grow plants (cornflowers, baby's-breath, blue lace flower, zinnias, China asters, scabiosa, dianthus, and more) in a cutting bed after the last frost in your area. (I counted 200 seedlings from one packet when I tried this several years ago but had to thin at least half of them out of a 4-foot-by-9-foot bed in the vegetable garden.) This is fun and enables you to learn the different plants, find out which ones grow well and which you want to grow again, and gather armloads of cut flowers while you are experimenting.

For earlier blooms, seeds can be started indoors and transplanted to the cutting garden later. When to sow them depends on how long they take to germinate and grow to transplanting size and on how much frost or cold weather the young plants can tolerate when they are moved to the garden. Under average home conditions, all you need to start your own plants from seed is a sunny windowsill in an east or south exposure or a place where indoor plant lights can be rigged. (Ordinary fluorescent tubes suspended just above the seed flats work well.) Also, a cold frame or enclosed porch is useful for hardening off plants, gradually exposing them to outdoor conditions, before putting them in the garden. For more detailed information, consult the general gardening sources in the Bibliography.

Annuals that self-sow freely—Shirley poppies, nicotiana, cleome, larkspur, petunias—are always welcome in the cutting garden. (Offspring of hybrid plants will not always look the same as the parent plant, however.) Some biennials—Newport Pink sweet William, canterbury bells, forget-me-nots, foxgloves, and pansies—are nice additions as well. These plants generally bloom the second year after they are sown, then die, although many have been developed to bloom the first year from an early sowing. You can achieve the effect of yearly bloom by planting a biennial in the garden two years in a row and allowing both plantings to self-sow.

THE
DOUBLE-DUTY
BORDER

The correct place for dill is the herb garden, but if you have not got a herb garden it will take a very decorative place in any border. I like muddling things up; and if an herb looks nice in a border, then why not grow it there? Why not grow anything anywhere so long as it looks right where it is? That is, surely, the art of gardening.

—*Vita Sackville-West*

A Joy of Gardening, 1958

ABOVE *Purple-tinged acanthus lends bold vertical strokes to the garden and to arrangements, but its handsome architectural foliage does not last long when cut.*

FACING PAGE *Blue spikes of Pacific Giants delphinium, dark red disks of Arabian Nights dahlias, and tiny white trumpets of nicotiana display striking contrasts in form and color, all neatly threaded together by gray and green foliage.*

PAGES 78—79 *Healthy, beautiful plants burgeon in a double border created by Glenn Withey and Charles Price in a Seattle suburb. Artful combinations of flowers and foliage and abundant planting typify the garden. A cutting garden lies toward the back of the property, but the borders could be picked for many bouquets without suffering.*

PAGE 79 *The lovely Aurelian lily Lilium 'Lady Anne' features flaring ivory flowers blended with apricot.*

A flower border is the centerpiece of a garden, no matter how large or small. No other garden feature receives the same attention lavished on flower beds and borders (except lawns, perhaps). Their main role is to adorn the garden throughout the season with shimmering colors and tossing shapes.

To say that flowers cut generously from a border will not be missed would be unrealistic. The damage can be kept within tolerable limits, however, so that the border, and the rest of the garden, retains its integrity as a decoration. This is easy if the border is turned to merely to supplement the pickings from a cutting garden. When the border is the main source for cut flowers, special care must be given to planning, planting, maintaining, and cutting from it to preserve its attractiveness. It is easier to gather blooms inconspicuously from a very large border or from several borders than from a single small border, but this problem is surmountable. The challenge is to create a satisfying border with a good color scheme that will provide flowers, foliage, and continuous change from spring through fall.

Flower borders have not always existed as we know them today. English gardener William Robinson, a "testy zealot," whose life spanned nearly a century from 1838 to 1935, railed against the Victorian fashion of bedding out tender annuals in garish colors in rigid geometric patterns and championed a more natural style of gardening. In 1883, in *The English Flower Garden*, Robinson called for using hardy perennial plants (those that survived and flourished in England's climate) and planting them in naturalistic masses in "long straight-sided beds," which he called "borders." He also espoused "mixed borders" of hardy perennials together with shrubs, trees, and other kinds of plants.

Robinson found a worthy ally in Gertrude Jekyll; the influence of these two people, more than any others, revolutionized gardening in the Western world. Jekyll, whose name is inexorably associated with the "English herbaceous border," transformed border making into a high art. In her lifetime (1843–1932), and often in

collaboration with the architect Sir Edwin Lutyens, she designed more than 300 borders, thoroughly exploring various plant combinations and color schemes.

Hardy herbaceous perennials have made the gardens of England famous for their abundance of bloom and beauty. The descendants of some of those plants grow in our gardens today, along with our own native species and modern cultivars.

Planning the Border

Before selecting perennials and other plants, the first priority is to find the best location for the border. As a more-or-less permanent feature in the garden, it deserves careful placement. You may want to enjoy looking out at it from the kitchen sink or while having a cool drink on the porch or terrace. Planted with a few small trees or shrubs, some of them evergreen, and grasses that turn into tawny sculptures in the winter garden, a border will be interesting even in the bleakest months. Where space permits, combining these plants with perennials, annuals, and bulbs will expand the seasonal interest of the border and will enrich your garden and your indoor decorations with branches, flowers, foliage, berries, and pods throughout the seasons.

While strolling the garden mulling over where to place a border, study the light and soil conditions of possible sites. (If you have drawn up a map of your property as discussed on page 32, this should be helpful now.) Look for a spot that receives a minimum of six hours of sun a day, has good drainage and a loose, friable soil. Soil can be amended up to a point; if there is a problem, someone on the staff of your county agricultural experimental station or a nearby botanic garden should be able to advise you.

If your property is heavily wooded, you will have to contend with shade. First, consider whether it is desirable and practical to prune tree branches to allow more light to reach the area where you would like to locate a border. In areas of light shade, or partial shade with some sun, you can still have an attractive and colorful border by selecting among the many

plants that either require some shade or will adapt nicely to it. Some woodland wildflowers such as bloodroot and trillium thrive under deciduous trees, blooming in spring before the canopy of leaves unfurls. Various lilies, Japanese roof iris (*Iris tectorum*), primulas, astilbe, ligularia, bleeding-heart, rodgersia, and a host of others grow well in shade. Expand your range of choices by including bulbs, annuals, perennials, shrubs, vines, and ground covers that tolerate low light.

If the area is fully shaded, you will have fewer plants to work with, but there may be compensating conditions such as moisture; the best approach is to experiment with different plants and see what works. (For more information on shade gardening, see the Bibliography.) Some of the loveliest indoor arrangements result from the ingenious use of a few flowers combined with attractive foliage from plants such as hostas and ferns that tolerate or thrive in shade.

Often, a place along a wall, fence, terrace, or hedge will cry out for a border. Ideally, such a backing should be tall enough to block out the far view so attention can be directed to the plants growing in front of it. Planting an evergreen vine such as ivy or a spreading euonymus at the foot of an ugly existing fence may make an acceptable backdrop. If no satisfactory backdrop exists, constructing a tall wooden fence of unbroken surface and painting it a neutral color is a superb and not necessarily expensive solution, especially if it also will block out an unsightly view.

A popular alternative to the one-sided border, island beds, championed most vigorously by England's plantsman Alan Bloom, are free-standing plantings usually surrounded by lawn; the shape can be rectangular but often follows a free-form design over the land. They can be perambulated and enjoyed from all sides. A distinctive hallmark of their design is the placement of the tallest plants in the middle to permit viewing and admiring the bed from all sides. Think of an island bed as being two borders placed back-to-back.

A border, or island bed, should fit comfortably with the house and the rest of the garden, echoing formality with straight lines, a rectangular shape, and a neat, controlled, and balanced planting, or it can sinuate over the garden in curved or free-form shapes to reinforce a mood of informality. A middle-of-the-road style, good in almost any setting, is to fashion the bed as a simple rectangle with straight sides and then allow the plants to billow seductively over the hard edges.

As for size, borders can run the gamut. Depending on how much space you have, a medium-sized border of, say, 30 feet by 10 feet can be successfully created as an attractive and productive double-duty border, to be augmented by picking from the rest of the garden. The usual advice is that the border should be in proportion to its surroundings, and that it should be twice as wide as the height of the tallest plant. But even

ABOVE *Red-hot-pokers* (Kniphofia *sp.*) *stand before a doorway. Their dense coral and cream flower spikes, ramrod straight, can be coaxed to curve during conditioning if a softer line is wanted for an arrangement.*

FACING PAGE, LEFT *Where space is ample, as it is in this remarkable garden in Katonah, New York, designed by the owner with a horticulturist who is also an artist, a large mixed border incorporating small trees, shrubs, perennials, and annuals holds richness and variety.*

FACING PAGE, RIGHT *An informal border follows the contour of the land at the André Viette Farm and Nursery in Fishersville, Virginia. The border displays plants that are grown and sold at the nursery and provides a decorative landscape for the owners who live on the property.*

ABOVE *Spider flower (Cleome hasslerana),
holds pride of place in this suburban Chicago
garden. White nicotiana, statice, prairie
gentian (Eustoma grandiflorum), and
silvery artemisia also grow in the bed.*

FACING PAGE *Flat umbels of pink yarrow
(Achillea millefolium) juxtaposed with
white panicles of phlox and small dangling
bells of lime green Nicotiana langsdorffii
present a trio of flower, form, and color.*

this depends on the plant's placement in the border—front, back, or
middle. While rules can be helpful
because they are the result of the accumulated experience of others, each
garden and the maker's vision of it is
unique, so trust your instincts.

If you have a small backyard and
want to grow as many flowers as it
will allow, consider sacrificing the
lawn. A paved central path flanked
by a double border shimmering with
soft colors and silver-foliaged plants,
or vibrant with red, yellow, and

look out of scale because a high rock ledge rising behind them minimizes their height.

Make the border wider than you think it should be, especially if you plan to include shrubs. This will give scope for grouping plants along its depth as well as length to create a lushness not possible if it is too narrow. Keep to a rectangular or oblong shape; square borders are harder to

A practical way to visualize the dimensions of a border is to outline a rectangular bed with stakes and string; for a curved border or free-form island bed, lay a garden hose or piece of rope on the ground along the desired shape. Study it from different angles, from inside the house, the terrace, the driveway, and so on, then adjust the size, shape, and orientation of the bed as needed. When

design and maintain. If possible leave about a two-foot path at the back of the planting; this minimizes root competition if the border is bounded by a hedge, allows air circulation, and provides access for maintenance. An edging of brick or stone along the front and level with the lawn will keep the grass at bay; make it wide enough to support one wheel of the lawnmower to ease cutting and edging. Also place stepping stones at strategic places in the border to avoid stepping on plant roots while you work.

you are satisfied, the area can be prepared for planting.

It's important to prepare the bed thoroughly in the beginning. While most will need dividing every few years, perennials are expected to grow in the same space in the border for many years. Turn the bed over in the fall and incorporate the appropriate amendments into it—peat moss, composted manure, and other decomposed organic material, as well as ground limestone, if a soil test shows that it is needed. The bed will settle by spring and be ready for planting.

orange daylilies and other sunny blooms, can provide great pleasure, as well as bouquets over many months.

The delphiniums at the back of one of my borders grow to about six feet, exactly the width of the border at that point. They do not

BELOW *A mood of spontaneity reigns in a mixed planting in front of a greenhouse in Oregon. Mophead hydrangeas and blue lily-of-the-Nile (*Agapanthus sp.*)— both superb candidates for cutting—will soon be joined here by masses of late summer asters and tall purple Joe-Pye weed (*Eupatorium purpureum).*

FACING PAGE *In this visual extravaganza in Seattle, the main players are blue* Campanula lactiflora *(in the background), tall* Lilium formosanum *'Queen Anne', golden yarrow, spiny sea holly (*Eryngium sp.*), drooping red trumpets of* Phygelius *'Devil's Tears', daylilies, gray-green leaflets of the lovely* Helleborus corsicus, *and the giant seed head of* Allium christophii.

Selecting the plants and deciding how to combine them artistically in the border can offer great pleasure. Allow your creativity and imagination full rein. Try to design the planting scheme over the less hectic winter months when there will be time for thoughtful planning and for savoring the process, which can be as much fun as concocting your indoor arrangements later.

Many experienced gardeners can "design" a border with a trowel in one hand and a plant in the other, if they are veterans who have accumulated a fair share of triumphs and defeats and through them have come to know plants intimately. A solid knowledge of plants is the basis of good gardening, but trial and error work over

time as well. Intelligent planning is equally valuable. Good gardeners tread each of these creative paths in different measure at different times. A few guidelines follow for those who wish to plot their design on paper before implementing it. Supplementary detailed instruction on creating borders is available in any number of garden books, some of which are listed in the Bibliography.

The Plant Profiles will help you to begin your plant list. You will also need a comprehensive illustrated plant encyclopedia. I recommend *Perennials for American Gardens,* by Ruth Rogers Clausen and Nicolas H. Ekstrom, supplemented with *The National Arboretum Book of Outstanding Garden Plants,* by Jacqueline Hériteau,

TOP *The satiny pink perennial* Sidalcea
malviflora *'Elsie Heugh' resembles an
elegant miniature hollyhock, is lovely in the
border when planted as a group, and is an
excellent cut flower. Kept cut, it will send
out a second flush of bloom.*

MIDDLE *Daylilies gracefully border a path
at historic Oatlands Plantation in Leesburg,
Virginia. These robust plants in wonderful
forms and colors deserve a place in formal
and informal gardens. Each flower lasts but
a day, but a mature plant may put up eight
or more branched scapes, each holding several
flowers for a long period of bloom. The
flowers are best used in informal bouquets in
which spent blooms may be removed without
ruining a structured effect. Open blooms
plucked for a luncheon may be laid directly
on the table, where they will last a day
without water.*

BOTTOM *A resplendent border encircles the
lawn at Heronswood Nursery, in Kingston,
Washington. Trees and shrubs, many of
them Asiatic species not commonly seen, give
structure to the border and backing for the
perennials spilling out in front. While the
Zone 8 climate of the Pacific Northwest
accommodates many plants that do not grow
in the Northeast, emphasis is being placed
increasingly on "water-wise" plants.*

TOP *A secluded resting place beckons in the cool shade of a* Magnolia × soulangiana, *perhaps the oldest on Chicago's North Shore. Oak-leaved hydrangea (*Hydrangea quercifolia*), witch hazel (*Hamamelis virginia*), and bergenia grow in the heavier shade, while* Echinacea *'Bright Star' and white* Lilium *'Olivia' push out on the sunnier fringe. The daylily* Hemerocallis *'Golden Chimes' provides a splash of color.*

MIDDLE *An opulent double border is planted right to the water's edge of a swimming pool on a New York estate. Architectural ornamental grasses and the exotic king-size leaves of elephant's-ear plant (*Alocasia *sp.) in the border on the right impart a lush tropical mood. Meticulous maintenance is required to keep the water free of plant debris.*

BOTTOM *The nonflowering lamb's-ears* Stachys byzantina *'Silver Carpet' is the catalyst in this pleasing triad. Its silvery foliage next to the yellow blooms of* Coreopsis *intensifies the color and texture, and sets off the daintier, lighter yellow blossoms of shrubby* Potentilla fruticosa. *The velvety leaves of lamb's-ears are useful in arrangements if conditioned first in warm water.*

THE DOUBLE-DUTY BORDER

89

which includes trees, shrubs, and grasses as well as annuals, perennials, bulbs, and vines. (For others, consult the Bibliography.) You will also want to send for mail-order nursery catalogs for ordering plants, as your local garden center probably will not carry every plant you want; many give helpful information.

PERENNIALS

Unlike in the cutting garden, where annuals reign, the mainstays of the border are perennial plants, whose flowers appear year after year. Some display an amazing tenacity for life. Some peonies, bearded irises, Oriental poppies, and bleeding-hearts, handed down through several generations, are still thriving. Actually, whether a plant is truly perennial in your climate or in the microclimate of your garden depends on its hardiness, hence the importance of ascertaining the hardiness of any perennial you plan to acquire. Delphiniums, for example, often last only two years in gardens in the Northeast, behaving almost as biennials. Perennials are multifaceted, with foliage and flowers in myriad shapes, textures, forms, and a wide palette of colors. Many are adapted to diverse situations; give them the soil, light, and moisture they need, and most will repay you by growing and multiplying lustily.

Perennials diverge from annuals in their survival strategies. Rather than putting all their energies into setting seed, perennials depend on their roots as a main survival mech-

anism. Their tops die back to the ground each winter, but with their life force safely underground, they are able to renew themselves each spring. As they grow, the original plants may increase in size by expanding outward or put out new satellite plants or runners—a bonus for the gardener.

HERBS

While considering different kinds of plants for beds and borders, leave room to include a few herbs for their variety and texture of foliage, their subtle colors, and their intoxicating fragrances when their leaves are touched or bruised. Although the charm and usefulness of these magical plants are legendary, and devotees grow them in patterned or knotted herb gardens edged with boxwood or lavender, we generally overlook their value in borders and in making fresh bouquets. Textures as different as the foliage of lacy artemisias, velvety peppermint geraniums, and rough and crisp sage and rosemary leaves will provide welcome contrasts in the border, in a centerpiece, or blended with other herbs and flowers in a bouquet or nosegay.

Herbs with gray or silvery foliage—artemisias, sages, and lamb's-ears, for example—create attractive accents. Skillfully chosen and threaded through the border, their clumps of platinum or washes of silver enliven and tie the planting together visually, especially during unplanned hiatuses between bloom times. Aside from its culinary uses,

ABOVE *Slender spikes of fragrant lavender grace a brick path in an herb garden.*

FACING PAGE, TOP *The double-duty border shown here, the central focus of the yard, yields many cut flowers as well. Useful for both roles are the red bee balm* Monarda didyma *'Mahogany', balloon flower (* Platycodon grandiflorus), *pink* Lilium *'Montreux' and 'Jet Star', the daylily* Hemerocallis *'Chicago Petticoats', and* Sedum *'Autumn Joy', not yet in bloom.*

FACING PAGE, BOTTOM LEFT *Daylilies in glorious colors can be planted in throngs for a succession of bloom. Cultivars may be selected to bloom from spring until frost, in sun or light shade, in soil with good drainage. A thousand new cultivars are introduced each year.*

FACING PAGE, BOTTOM RIGHT *Daylilies also mingle well with many other perennials, such as low-growing* Coreopsis verticillata *'Zagreb' and blue globe thistle (* Echinops ritro).

RIGHT *Five species of lavender mingle their scent with those of santolina, mint, and dozens of other medicinal and culinary herbs in a restored early American herb garden. Blooming in the outer borders are silverleaved Russian sage (*Perovskia atriplicifolia*), the bee balm Monarda didyma 'Croftway Pink', yarrow, and tall plume poppy (*Macleaya cordata*).*

BELOW, LEFT *The herb fennel (*Foeniculum vulgare*), which may grow to six feet, has lacy sulfur umbels that are attractive in the border and excellent as cut flowers.*

BELOW, RIGHT *Foliage, flowers, and seedpods from these herbs are dried and used in arrangements by the garden's owner, Georgia Vance, an author and authority on dried flowers. Woven here into beds of luminous textures are teucrium, gray and green santolina, lamb's-ears, sage, lavender, rosemary, silver thyme, and other herbs.*

FACING PAGE *Ruby red pelargoniums, with variegated leaves, silky Silver Mound artemisia, and lamb's-ears enliven a bed edged with boxwood. Pelargoniums, often overlooked as cut flowers, offer wonderful colors and substantial round shapes for bouquets.*

curly or even flat-leaf parsley serves well as an emerald green edging to the border (pick outside stems and it will replenish itself from the center), furnishes greenery for bouquets, and makes a fine ruff collar around a bunch of marigolds or daisies. Basil, too, lends a good green to the border and is a fragrant filler with cut flowers. The tantalizing airiness of feathery dill and bronze fennel is invaluable, and tricolor sage and purple-leaved perilla (*Perilla frutescens* 'Atropurpurea') make superb focal plants whether planted or arranged with other herbs or cut flowers in water.

Some herbs can be dried for use in arrangements, wreaths, and potpourri; other graceful spikes of tiny blooms, lacy flower heads, or tightly packed round inflorescences (such as chive blossoms) lend a piquant delicacy to bouquets. The best way to

ABOVE, LEFT *A quadrant of a well-designed and generously furnished flower garden features clematis in the center of a diamond-shaped bed. The beds and surrounding borders present a sensual feast of color, fragrance, and textures. As in all good gardens, there is constant flux as annuals, perennials, and shrubs wax and wane.*

ABOVE, RIGHT *Red and yellow are strong colors, but used together here in moderation, the effect is exhilarating and nonclashing. Brilliant scarlet flower clusters of Maltese cross (*Lychnis chalcedonica*) are the first to attract attention. The yellowish-green bracts of spurge (*Euphorbia sp.*) are less dominating, and the lavender and purple hues of buddleia and salvia, together with green and grayish foliage, are the peacemakers.*

acquaint yourself, or to expand your relationship, with this admirable group is to make them inhabitants in your garden on a long-term (perennial), short-term (annual), or biennial basis.

The Matter of Color

Some gardeners seem to have a knack for combining colors with unfailing flair, yet can't explain how they do it. The rest of us plod along, trying to understand color theories, making notes when we see a combination we like either in a book or in somebody else's garden, and often end up making a color decision as gardeners have always done: taking the flowering plant to the garden and studying its color and shape by holding it against other plants until a compatible companion is found. There is much to explore regarding color; anyone wishing to pursue this matter could do no better than to begin with Gertrude Jekyll's *Colour Schemes for the Flower Garden*, written in 1908

(now available as a reissue) and still the bible on this subject. (Also see the Bibliography.)

If the idea of studying color theories is intimidating, yet you want to have a better color sense that can be translated into prettier plantings and bouquets, start simply. Pick a few flowers in your favorite colors and put them in a jug of water; then rearrange them and decide which combinations you like best. Try working with all soft colors at first, perhaps using all roses in various shades of pink and white; then add deeper shades: reds, burgundies, and so on.

For another bouquet, select only dark-colored flowers to work with, or all of one color—blues, possibly—in different shades and tints. (Shades are darker than the hue; tints lighter.) Then try expanding the color range by including various flowers in many colors; observe the different effects you get each time. You will discover what color combinations appeal to you, and you can

ABOVE, LEFT *Sulfur yellow flower heads of fennel and light blue* Campanula lactiflora *are mutually enhancing in this classic color combination.*

ABOVE, RIGHT *Clumps of red and yellow flowers repeated at rhythmic intervals along the border give it coherence.*

LEFT *Purple violas mingle with foliage as fascinating as any flower.*

Soft warm tones permeate this combination of plants. The muted coppery tones of a sedge (Carex *sp.*) are echoed in the light peach daylilies, the yellow fennel flower clusters blend subtly, and wine-colored drumstick alliums inject a pleasing accent.

Bright yellow yarrow, chartreuse lady's-mantle, and vivid pink Dianthus deltoides *create an intense but effective color combination.*

The golden central blush and orange anthers of white species lilies (Lilium formosanum) *pick up the rich yellow and orange of* Helenium autumnale *blooming at their feet.*

Slender sheaves of Pennisetum *sp.* link the salmon pink flower heads of yarrow (Achillea millefolium) *with a mass of daisies. The green foliage also neutralizes a possible clash between the yarrow and mauve pink loosestrife (Lythrum sp.).*

White snapdragons highlight the orange flower clusters of butterfly weed (Asclepias tuberosa), *while gray, broad-leaved lamb's-ears (Stachys byzantina) enhances both.*

The gray architecture of Scotch thistle (Onopordum *sp.) brings out the best in pearl pink dahlias and milky blue* Campanula lactiflora.

*Shaggy shasta daisy (*Leucanthemum × superbum*) paired with false sunflower (*Heliopsis helianthoides*) and* Lobelia tupa *present a cheerful combination.*

In this pleasing vignette, the rich yellow of daisies is continued, but more softly, by spiky verbascum above, while white trumpet lilies reiterate the purple and pink notes of the salvias.

A symphony in pink is created by silky blooms of Sidalcea *sp. and pinkish white bracts of* Salvia sclarea. *Opening globes of* Allium giganteum *'Rosy Giant' will add mauve pink florets to the composition.*

Pink foxglove, coral lupine, and red and yellow columbine work well in this combination of color and form.

*Pink and blue are effective partners, as seen in pink roses (*Rosa *'The Fairy'), blue larkspur, and bright blue hardy ageratum (*Eupatorium coelestinum*), which appears here as lilac.*

These lovely plants could comprise a fragrant white garden: white Phlox paniculata, *white spotted Oriental lily, tuberose (*Polianthes tuberosa*), and pale pinkish white* Veronicastrum virginicum.

then repeat these patterns in your garden. Of course, texture and form also play a role, and experimenting with flowers in a container is not the same as working with larger garden plantings, but such experiments will help you sharpen your natural eye for color. Notice the natural color beauty that is all around—in fields, at the shore, in evening sunsets— and store them up for inspiration when gardening and arranging.

Color theories have been devised with the use of a wheel to show the interrelationships of colors. If you are timid about your own color sense, these help to sort out which combinations are generally pleasing and which are not.

On the color wheel, the primary colors, blue, yellow, and red, are placed in triangular fashion. Other colors resulting from blending the three primary colors are shown in proper sequence on the wheel. By dividing the color wheel in half, with the axis running through red and green, the "warm" colors are on one side and the "cool" colors are on the other. You can mix together any of the colors on one side and get a harmonious effect because they share a common hue. Thus, warm colors (scarlet, orange, yellow, and yellow-green) share yellow while cool colors (crimson, violet, blue, and blue-green) share blue.

You can also combine colors that are directly opposite each other on the color wheel. Such complementary colors do not have a hue in common; they intensify each other,

creating vibrant matches, such as dark blue salvia fronted by orange butterfly weed.

Another possibility (not a recommendation) is to combine colors that are obliquely opposite each other. Generally, such contrasting color schemes, combining plants of any two or all three of the primary colors, tend to jar and overwhelm, and would be especially disastrous in a small border. Combine red, blue, and yellow with other colors in the

ABOVE *Pure white phlox is an effective counterpoint in an effusive planting of pinks, reds, and yellows.*

FACING PAGE, TOP *Scintillating red astilbes draw the eye first in this border planned for continuous color over a long season. Low-growing gray-foliaged plants harmonize the brighter colors; the red and-white theme changes to pastels, orange, and blue farther along the border.*

FACING PAGE, BOTTOM *A purple ornamental cabbage sets aglow the red poppies and blanket flower (Gaillardia × grandiflora). The silver-leaved helichrysum in the upper left highlights the grayish cast of the cabbage. Cabbage leaves, conditioned overnight to remove the smell, are stunning in arrangements.*

border, or place plants in these strong colors off by themselves. Red, in particular, is a difficult color in the garden, and a little goes a long way. On the other hand, you might appreciate the excitement it brings. A mass of clear red wiry sprays of *Crocosmia* 'Lucifer' can sing out as a stunning counterpoint in the border or in a bouquet. If clashes occur between contrasting colors, add green- or gray-foliage plants between the offending parties. These are notable peacemakers in the garden and will

often neutralize the dissonance; however, silvery gray foliage next to some reds will make them more vibrant.

Done with flair, other color contrasts sometimes work. "Few would agree," says Pamela Harper in *Designing with Perennials*, "that orange and magenta are harmonious, but some enjoy the excitement of an occasional raucous note." Bright orange poppies peeping through *Lychnis coronaria* offer just the right touch of impudence.

The simplest color scheme for a border is to focus on one color, say, blue (or white, as in the fabled White Garden at Sissinghurst) and combine plants in that hue with other plants in its varying shades and tints. Contrary to popular practice, this does not mean that all other colors should be excluded. White lilies, or a flower of the palest lemon-yellow, sensitively placed in a blue garden will heighten the blues. The same effect is seen when soft yellow snapdragons mingle with blue campanulas in an indoor arrangement.

At the other extreme is the spirited border of many colors, like Joseph's coat. In it, random couplings of color, usually by an inexperienced gardener, can produce "a terrible if joyous racket" (as Louise Beebe Wilder aptly observed). Its saving grace is that it allows the gardener to discover what works, what doesn't, and to repeat in later years the happy accidents that occasionally result.

Colors also can trick the eye: cool colors appear to retreat into the background, warm colors to advance. It is possible to create spatial distor-

tions with plants to make the border
or the garden appear either larger or
smaller. For example, blue flowers of
caryopteris on the garden's perimeter will appear to magnify the distance; yellow daylilies or sunflowers
will "come forward" to shorten it.
Colors can be manipulated to evoke
certain emotions—cool colors can
calm, soothe; warm colors can excite,
shout. These are but some of the
general approaches to using color in
gardens and in the border. Select the

plants that flower in the colors you
favor when you want them. Also
check catalogs for details.

In the end, there is no use in
being dogmatic about color theory,
especially in dealing with "living
colors" as we gardeners do. So many
permutations are possible. Growing
conditions can change a plant's color.
In a single minute, a color can look
washed out in sunlight, intensified
by cloud cover. Plant colors change
with the seasons and within the life
cycle of each plant as flowers and

leaves open and fade. Texture, proportion, and setting also influence
color. And personal preferences and
reactions make color a highly sub-
jective matter.

Designing with Plants

After you have chosen a dominant
color scheme, note the heights and
bloom times of each plant on your
list, then divide them into categories
according to season: spring, summer,
midsummer, autumn. This will enable you to place them in groups
in the border, massing the plants
in color combinations so that as
one group of plants stops blooming, ideally another will be coming
into flower. It will be easier if you
will limit yourself to several favorites
for each season, and mass each kind
in groups of three, five, or seven
plants, depending on their mature
size and available space. Keep in
mind that achieving continuity of
color throughout the growing season requires a large border; at least
try to have your border look its best

A classical urn provides the focal point for a formal double border in Lake Forest, Illinois. The color scheme centers on yellow, white, and pink, with a few blue accents, and the colors are repeated at regular intervals along the border. Tall white and yellow lilies are positioned at a crosswalk halfway down the border. The perennials bloom prodigiously over a long period and include yarrow, loosestrife, Sedum 'Autumn Joy', rudbeckia, phlox, chrysanthemums, and dahlias. Divisions of favorite perennials go into the cutting garden.

during the times you are there to enjoy it. Then make a plan to scale of the dimensions of the border on graph paper, using a scale of either ½ inch or ¼ inch to a foot. Lay tracing paper over this for working out plant combinations for the border; later, you can transfer your final design to the graph paper.

Getting the colors right for each season of bloom will take some fussing. Working on tracing paper, strive for a balanced composition for every season, weaving the colors throughout the border. Include a group or so of spring flowering bulbs and reli-

able annuals to extend the season and ensure color; select varieties also good for cutting.

The tallest plants are generally placed at the back of the border, with shorter ones in front for a comfortable sense of balance. But avoid the monotonous rigidity of a step-stool effect by placing here and there along the border a tall, airy plant such as thalictrum or baby's-breath in front of a shorter plant for a surprise effect.

Play with shapes, juxtaposing spiky blooms with softer, rounded forms. Contrast foliage textures as well, perhaps placing the glossy, dark

green leaves of peonies with the lacy, fernlike foliage of *Achillea* 'Moonshine'. Plant silver- and gray-foliaged plants—the subshrub Russian sage (*Perovskia atriplicifolia*) is a choice mid-border favorite—at intervals through the border for unity and rhythm.

Make maximum use of space to assure extra blooms for picking. Allow room to plant vining plants—clematis, sweet pea, or the annual cup-and-saucer vine (*Cobaea scandens*) —to climb up through the sprays of Russian sage and scamper over the branching arms of the everblooming Bonica rose (*Rosa* 'Meidomonac') or

R. 'The Fairy', both four-star cutting roses. Plant seedlings of biennial wallflowers (started in the cold frame or nursery area the previous year) between tulips; when these are spent, pull out the wallflowers and fill in with fast-growing annuals. (I also gather self-sown seedlings of perilla, feverfew, and other volunteers from elsewhere in the garden and transplant them in the vacancies.)

Last, depart from conventional gardening wisdom by adding an extra plant or two at the foot of each kind you fancy for arranging. This double planting will enable the border to fulfill its two-pronged function without sacrificing appearances.

Afterthoughts

It will take at least two years for perennial plants to grow and fit comfortably into their allotted spaces in the border. Annual plants—snapdragons, *Salvia farinacea* 'Victoria', airy cosmos, and others that also make superb cut flowers—can fill in the gaps in the meantime, as well as provide nonstop color. A border planted generously to serve the dual role of ornament and cutting bed will require additional doses of nutrients if the plants are to thrive and flower; an extra handful of composted manure applied to each plant midseason should adequately supplement a heavier spring feeding of an organic fertilizer or a topdressing of aged manure in early spring. Using too much of fertilizers that are rich in nitrogen can produce lush foliage, weak stems, and few flowers.

Squeezing the optimal number of plants into the double-duty border can be problematic: too few and the house will suffer, too many and the plants may suffer. You will have to find and maintain the balance; each situation is different. Be vigilant during humid weather for signs of disease that could result because of lack of good air circulation. At the first sign of mildew or other attack, take appropriate action, using biological or biodegradable sprays where there is an option. Sometimes, the best course is to pull up infected plants and discard them (*not* on the compost pile).

If the soil has been adequately prepared, aside from the usual maintenance, such as staking and dividing, the only other tasks required will be to water in times of drought, deadhead spent flowers that lived out the season in the flower bed, and cut down and cart away mushy stalks after frost. The border will require constant fine-tuning, however, as Vita Sackville-West advised: "Gardening is largely a question of mixing one sort of plant with another sort of plant, and of seeing how they marry happily together; and if you see that they don't marry happily, then you must hoick one of them out and be quite ruthless about it" (*A Joy of Gardening*, 1958). Otherwise, cut blossoms and leaves for your house generously but discreetly. As the border evolves and changes, it will continue to provide flowers and joy, which is all we can ask of it.

MEADOWS AND ORNAMENTAL GRASSES

Modified Meadow Gardens

Ornamental Grasses

ABOVE *Many daisy-type flowers such as these sunny yellow tickseed* (Coreopsis) *are superb for meadow plantings, offering easy growing, non-stop blooms over a long period.*

FACING PAGE *Instead of a lawn to mow there are flowers to pick in a prairie garden surrounding a weekend retreat in Lake Forest, Illinois. Yellow coneflowers, small white fleabane* (Erigeron sp.), *purple coneflower* (Echinacea purpurea), *and Queen-Anne's-lace can be gathered freely without making a dent in the display.*

PAGES 104–105 *Jaunty black-eyed Susan, Queen-Anne's-lace, and silvery artemisia— with more to come in the background—fringe a meadow on floral designer Renny Reynolds' Bucks County farm in Pennsylvania.*

PAGE 105 *Most of the tall ornamental grasses—related to lawn grasses—begin to flower in late summer, offering spiky plumes and intriguing seed heads for arrangements.*

A meadow holds special charms. Waves of sun-drenched flowers and graceful grasses sway in the breeze; birds, butterflies, crickets, and other denizens of the wild make it their home. Suddenly, there is sound, movement, change. And myriad wildings—Johnny-jump-ups, daisies, buttercups, bachelor's-buttons, Queen-Anne's-lace, bouncing Bet— can be gathered for innocent bouquets. For those gardeners who experiment with innovative ways of labor-saving gardening, creating a meadow garden is a viable option. A meadow garden, or prairie garden in the Midwest, is a low-maintenance, naturalistic planting that is a good alternative to a lawn—or to part of it. It offers a way to break away from the weekend routine of mowing, blowing, fertilizing, liming, watering, aerating, and other coddling required to keep a lawn the prized greensward of the neighborhood. Once established, a meadow will require little upkeep and virtually no supplemental watering, fertilizer, or pest or disease control measures.

A successful meadow planting can serve as an astonishing source for cut flowers. If you are bewitched (as I am) by roadside wildflowers such as Queen-Anne's-lace, oxeye daisy, and chicory, you can grow them in your own patch. These, as well as butterfly weed, asters, goldenrod, Joe-Pye weed, and other "weedy" plants are perfectly appropriate for a customized meadow. Grow them from seed (or purchase seedlings from reputable wildflower nurseries), and you can pick blossoms for bouquets with a clear conscience that you have left their populations in the wild intact.

Don't be afraid to expand your choices to the many other wonderful tough, hardy, and long-lived perennials that are also grown in borders and which are utterly delightful in casual indoor displays: yarrow, purple coneflower, coreopsis, black-eyed Susan, monarda, heliopsis, lysimachia, liatris, sedum 'Autumn Joy', for example. A scattering of easy, self-sowing annuals and noninvasive grasses will bring even more color and richness to the meadow and, when cut, to country jugs and simple vases.

The seeming randomness of a

meadow can be misleading. To create a meadow demands more than scratching out some lawn or other piece of ground, scattering seeds of a meadow mix over it, and waiting for nature to take its course. This approach will result in a meadow entangled with every kind of opportunistic weed in the neighborhood —poison ivy, honeysuckle, chokecherry, mugwort, crabgrass, and their legions. A good deal of effort and shrewd timing is required at the start. It would be prudent to begin on a small scale: put in a test plot first in the corner of the lawn, or as an island bed; when the results are in, the meadow can be gradually enlarged. With patience, a meadow can be successfully established over three or four years.

Modified Meadow Gardens

In "stylizing" a mini-meadow, or a larger one, for your property, you will have some control over the direction you want it to take. This will depend on your tastes and preferences, how strong a part you want to play in its development, and your willingness to accept its natural spontaneity.

Should you decide to turn over some part of your front acreage to meadow or create a meadow that will be on view to neighbors and passersby, check first with your local town or city officials. Some areas have weed-control, fire-prevention, or building-code ordinances that might apply; if so, you must gain permission before you begin.

Meadows can be created on dry

or moist soils with good drainage. (Adding generous quantities of compost to heavy soils often will improve drainage; check with the agency where your soil was tested.) Full sun, at least six hours a day, is crucial. The soil shouldn't be too rich in nutrients, which will cause weak, ungainly plants with succulent foliage and sparse flowering. Amend the soil to improve the tilth, rather than fertilize, by mixing in aged manure, decomposed leaves, peat moss, or other organic materials.

Select your plants or seeds with care, matching their cultural requirements with the intended meadow area. Study the wild places in your neighborhood to see what grows naturally. You needn't limit yourself strictly to native North American wildflowers; mix native plants and unfussy cultivated ones. Include some annuals to give you color the first year—cosmos, cleome, baby-blue-eyes, annual coreopsis, field poppies, bachelor's-buttons. Some will self-seed, but usually they peter out by the third year. Add small and medium-sized clumping grasses such as quaking grass (*Briza media*, to three feet), little bluestem (*Schizachyrium scoparium*, to five feet), blue oat grass (*Helictotrichon sempervirens*, to five feet), and the popular dwarf fountain grass (*Pennisetum alopecuroides* 'Hameln', to three feet). These all are well behaved and provide graceful flower panicles and unique seed pods for fresh and dried arrangements.

Seed companies and native plant and prairie restoration groups all

offer seeds and information. State highway departments, working with conservationists, have done research on meadow plantings along roadways. They can be valuable resources. Contact your state highway engineering department and plant societies

to find out what has worked in your area.

If you already have an area on your property that has naturalized through neglect (but is not yet a jungle), this might provide a good head start for a customized meadow. You could dig out patches and plug in started seedlings of native plants or divisions of tough, long-blooming plants from the flower garden, giving them plenty of room to grow and spread; or plant seeds in the pockets. Mark the pockets with tall

Aside from the showier cultivars of hardy plants, rattlesnake master, ironweed, and big and little bluestem grasses are among the native wildflowers and grasses that grow in a reclaimed prairie garden in Illinois. The prairie—basically a meadow in a dry area of the country—spreads over ten acres and is virtually maintenance-free, except for an annual burning.

ABOVE *Clumps of* Miscanthus sinensis *and the slightly shorter fountain grass (*Pennisetum alopecuroides*) lend structure and interest to a cutting garden on a Virginia estate. In late summer, their plumy inflorescences and seed heads are ready for picking.*

FACING PAGE, TOP *A low-maintenance garden, the result of good design and sensitivity to the environment, flows along a hillside in Vancouver, Washington. Shown here is one of a pair of borders planted with undemanding ornamental grasses and rugged perennials. Plumes of flowering* Calamagrostis acutiflora *glow in the background, lush arching mounds of* Pennisetum alopecuroides *border the lawn, and spiky* Veronicastrum virginicum *bows in the foreground.*

FACING PAGE, BOTTOM *Ornamental grasses play a major role in another garden in Vancouver, Washington. The tall grasses give vertical structure and provide a green framework against which smokebush (*Cotinus coggygria*), spider flower (*Cleome hasslerana*), and other plants display their colorful flowers.*

stakes so that you can find them to monitor their progress. Apply a thick mulch around the plants or seed pockets to keep down invasive weeds and conserve water; salt hay is a good choice because it is weed-free. This approach allows you to plant only what you can manage at one time and to expand the meadow gradually until it attains the appearance you want.

The other way to prepare for a meadow is to clear, till, and sow an entire area. Existing weeds and sod must be removed from the area to give new seedlings a chance to grow without competition. This is difficult and tricky because weed seeds can lie dormant in the soil for years; if disturbed and brought to the

surface by tilling, they will germinate, grow, and take over the whole meadow. Count on it. When it comes to survival of the fittest, noxious weeds have no peers.

There are a couple of ways to handle this task. A small area can be covered with black plastic for several months to smother the vegetation. Or it can be cleared by hand, then disked or tilled lightly (by hand or Rototiller). Tilling is repeated several times at two- or three-week intervals to kill any new weeds that germinate. Some experts advise deep tilling in fall followed by shallow tilling in the spring before sowing. Or you can use an herbicide such as Roundup, which is said to be harmless to humans, other animals, and soil if used with care and according to specific instructions.

Even if you are thorough in preparing and sowing a meadow garden, and do not neglect mulching and watering the area well during the first months, light weeding will still be necessary for the first year or two until the plants you started grow to cover all the bare spots. Grub out any woody seedlings forthwith, and if no rain falls for several weeks, provide water. After about the third year, you will be able to relax for the most part and enjoy what you and nature will have wrought.

An annual mowing will be necessary to keep a meadow healthy and to disperse the seeds of spent flowers so that it can perpetuate itself. (To help this process, leave a decent number of your favorite flowers uncut.) Mowing, with a cutter bar or scythe, can be done in late fall after a killing frost in the Northeast, but part of the joy of having a meadow is its presence in the winter landscape: flower heads heavy with snow, tawny grasses still holding seed stalks against the sky or dancing in the wind. Thus, it's nice to know that the job can be put off until earliest spring, before the ground turns to mush and the meadow comes alive again.

Ornamental Grasses

In the United States, the use of ornamental grasses as decorative elements in gardens waxed and waned until about the late 1970s, when interest burgeoned. An enterprising nur-

seryman in Baltimore, Kurt Bluemel, responded to the demand and began making available a wide range of ornamental grasses. At about the same time, the innovative work of two landscape architects, in the Washington, D.C., area, Wolfgang Oehme and James van Sweden, was attracting attention. In place of lawns and traditional borders, the two men covered the ground with groups of stately ornamental grasses, such as

Miscanthus and Pennisetum species and varieties, intermingled with large masses of rudbeckia 'Goldsturm', sedum 'Autumn Joy', yarrow (both 'Moonshine' and 'Coronation Gold'), and other sturdy perennials. Their low-maintenance style of gardening, referred to as the New American Garden, is described in the book by the same name written by Carole Ottesen. (See the Bibliography.)

The influence of Oehme and van

Sweden, and the ever-increasing new varieties of grasses that are being offered, have brought ornamental grasses into the gardening mainstream. This widens our options for landscaping and arranging material, and challenges our imagination to use them creatively.

Before perennial ornamental grasses became prominent in home gardens, the grasses used in indoor arrangements were chiefly the annuals. Their main value has been as dried, often dyed, additions to winter bouquets along with other flowers that dry easily, commonly known as immortelles or everlastings. With few exceptions, mainly the smaller, low-growing plants with big flowers, annual grasses have weedy-looking foliage and are not first-class border subjects.

Botanically, grasses belong to the Poacea, the most important plant family on earth as a source of food, since it encompasses the cereal grasses—wheat, corn, oats, barley, and other grains. Informally, grasses include not only true grasses but grasslike rushes, sedges, and cattails, which belong to separate families. Members of this extended group, sometimes called "the grudges," have bladelike narrow leaves and reduced flowers without petals, which are wind-pollinated.

Grasses hold their flowering stems high above the plant itself to catch air currents; when backlit by the sun, the inflorescences and foliage can appear luminescent. Back- or sidelit wine red blades of Japanese blood grass (*Imperata cylindrica* 'Red Baron') are the most stunning example; but all grasses should be oriented to take advantage of this fillip.

Some grasses put up substantial feathery plumes and spikes; slender stems of others, such as feather grasses (*Stipa* spp.), are lined with fine, fuzzy inflorescences and suspended above the leaves like skywriting waiting to disperse in the air. Their flowers are never garish but come in various muted hues of white, pink, gold, mauve, purple, or brown. The variety of colors,

textures, shapes, and patterned arrangements of flowers and seedpods on arching or upright stems become design elements for arrangers.

In the garden, grasses are valued for their ornamental foliage and flowers, and for the extended interest these features lend to the fall and winter landscape. (However, those of tropical origin will not survive in northern climates.) Many hardy grasses will bloom gloriously toward the end of summer, then pick up the autumnal theme by turning to hay shades of gold, parchment, and ochre, and remain throughout winter as attractive accents in the garden. But where summers are cool, damp, or short and where winter comes early, some grasses never flower and do not show fall color.

Grasses can be used in mixed borders, as individual focal points or accent plants, massed by themselves or with other grasses. Measuring from a few inches in height to many feet, they can be put to use as low ground covers and edgings or tall screening hedges. There are grasses for wet and dry soils. Basic shapes are upright, arching, clumping, or hummocks. The invasive stoloniferous ones, those with running roots, such as ribbon grass (*Phalaris arundinacea*), are good only as ground covers.

Foliage comes in hues of many shades of green, cream, gold, silver, variegated, brown, purplish, and red, generally muted. Grasses are subdued, touchable plants of gentle demeanor, even the 12-foot giant ravenna grass (*Erianthus ravennae*)

and tall moor grass *Molinia caerulea* 'Skyracer'. Put them where you can watch their alluring, rhythmic swaying in a breeze or hear the sound of their dried sheaves rustling in an autumn wind.

Varieties are numerous, and my experience centers around the familiar ones. I planted *Miscanthus sinensis* 'Gracillimus' about ten years ago, when only several varieties of maiden grass were being offered, and perhaps only a dozen of other grasses.

ABOVE *If not cut back until early spring, ornamental grasses lend a presence to the winter garden when there is little else to look out on, as here in the author's garden in late January. Many grasses hold their seed heads long into the winter, and they can be picked as needed.*

FACING PAGE *Along with evergreen trees and shrubs, ornamental grasses such as these tawny clumps of maiden grass (*Miscanthus sinensis *'Gracillimus'*) are valuable assets in the sparse landscape of late autumn.*

Others in my garden are the dwarf fountain grass (*Pennisetum alopecuroides* 'Hameln'), ravenna grass (*Erianthus ravennae*), ribbon grass (*Phalaris arundinacea* 'Picta'), Japanese blood grass (*Imperata cylindrica* 'Red Baron'), blue fescue (*Festuca ovina* var. *glauca*), and feather reed grass (*Calamagrostis* × *acutiflora* 'Karl Foerster').

The late-blooming flowering stalks of maiden, fountain, and ravenna grass have all been good performers in fresh and dried arrangements. I use them with the sturdy perennials they look good with in the garden, and which bloom at the same time—Autumn Joy sedum, Morden's Pink loosestrife, yarrow, purple coneflower, Joe-Pye weed, and, of course, *Rudbeckia fulgida* var. *sullivantii* 'Goldsturm'. I have not tried them with annuals. I have not brought ribbon grass into the house, though I think its graceful, variegated cream-and-green blades could help out in bouquets that need softening by slender arching lines. And the burgundy foliage of Japanese blood grass could look dazzling in many combinations using white, pink, blue, gold, or red blooms.

If I had room for only one ornamental grass, I would choose Karl Foerster's feather reed grass (*Calamagrostis* × *acutiflora* 'Karl Foerster'), the ultimate flowering grass, dubbed by Foerster himself as "metamorphic." In mid-June, it shoots strong, wiry stems four feet into the air, tipped with fluffy pink flowers that, from a distance, look like giant astilbes. The hazy pink inflorescences turn to dark amethyst by midsummer and mature to narrow golden spikes by fall, about the time that the green fountain of foliage also takes on a golden hue. In the East, it will grow to five or six feet; even one clump will make a fabulous accent in the garden, and you can cut in succession three colors of flowers.

Sedges, too, offer leaves and flowering plumes for arrangements if you can give them the moist shady conditions they prefer. Two choice ones are *Carex elata* 'Bowles Golden', a chartreuse-variegated sedge; and *C. morrowii* 'Variegata', a silver-variegated Japanese sedge.

I have never grown bamboos, which are true grasses, but I appreciate the impressive verdure they add to plantings, and admire them in arrangements. The canes are especially valuable for Japanese-style designs. (To condition bamboo foliage for a two-week vase life, submerge it in cold water until it is crisp.) However, most bamboos are notoriously invasive. Purportedly, the clumping kinds (though expensive) are noninvasive; *Sinarundinaria nitida* and *Thamnocalamus spathaceus* are two species reputed to be well behaved.

You can learn much about these dramatic plants by visiting public gardens across the country, especially botanic gardens and parks, where grasses, sedges, and bamboos are displayed in mixed plantings and all-of-a-kind groups. Take a camera and a notebook to record fresh ideas that can be adapted to the home landscape.

ABOVE *Scotch thistle* (Onopordum acanthium), *a biennial that self-sows and grows to nine feet tall, adapts well to meadow gardens. Its white or purple flower heads are useful in arrangements and easy to air-dry.*

FACING PAGE, TOP *A stunning clump of metallic blue-bladed grass, a native California species, joins the sundial as the focal point in this California flower garden. Its distinctive foliage is a fine complement for the pastel pink flower heads of yarrow* (Achillea millefolium) *blooming against it, and the tall wands of spiky flowers impart an airiness to the entire scene, as they will indoors in an arrangement.*

FACING PAGE, BOTTOM *The yarrow* Achillea filipendulina *'Gold Plate' and* Miscanthus sinensis *'Variegatus' are a classic plant combination. Both are sturdy, undemanding, and attractive plants that dress up the garden for several months.*

MEADOWS AND ORNAMENTAL GRASSES

115

ENJOYING
FLOWERS
INDOORS

Cutting Flowers

Conditioning

Flower Arranging

When arranging flowers . . . you must be ruthless with them.
Flowers should be hit and punched and strangled into shape. It is useless to
drift round the house with a lily in one hand and a geranium in the other,
and a Mona Lisa smile on your lips. . . . You must put on thick leather
gloves and jam them in and curse them under your breath.
—*Beverley Nichols*
Down the Garden Path, *1932*

ABOVE *A traditional arrangement using delphiniums, larkspur, cosmos, and roses beautifully complements a nineteenth-century Sèvres wine cooler and picks up its pink and blue colors.*

FACING PAGE *The last annuals from the author's cutting garden—snapdragons, mealy-cup sage, and zinnias—will mingle with heather, veronica, and other pickings in a colorful late summer bouquet.*

PAGES 116–117 *Gorgeous peonies flaunt their beauty in a simple, clear glass container, which permits a glimpse of the handsome stems as well.*

PAGE 117 *No flowering shrub outclasses the aristocratic tree peony for garden or arrangements. Its woody stems do not die to the ground in winter as do those of the herbaceous peony, and any pruning should be minimal.*

If your cut flowers have been grown in good soil under stress-free conditions, without excessive water and nitrogen (which, along with too much shade, produces leggy plants and weak blossoms), you will have blooms with good color, strong stems, and pleasing form to give your floral displays a strong head start. Not only are healthy cut flowers good keepers, but fresh plant material is the basis for appealing bouquets. Faded wilting flowers and shriveled foliage are not a pretty sight, no matter how skillfully arranged.

After flowers are cut, emphasis shifts to preventing the loss of moisture from their tissues for as long as possible. About three-fourths of a plant's weight is water, which it requires to carry on its life functions. You must supply this vital need to cut stems if you expect to keep them for any length of time; neglect it and many will perish with alarming speed.

Flowers that have been conditioned in water after being cut will look fresher and last longer in bouquets than those that have not undergone this step. And the fewer flowers the garden holds for cutting, the more important the matter of their longevity becomes; one then tends to be thrifty with blooms and wants to enjoy them as long as possible.

Even with adequate moisture and proper conditioning, flowers that have been cut from the parent plant differ in how long they will last, just as their life-spans vary in the garden. The sumptuous blooms of the southern magnolia (*Magnolia grandiflora*) will collapse virtually overnight, while most daisylike flowers will stay fresh for more than a week, and foliage such as that of ivy or galax may last for several weeks. The yardstick for measuring freshness varies as well. For some gardeners, when the flower color fades, it is a signal to toss them out. Others wait until petals fall or foliage wilts, or all of the above. A different situation exists when a single stalk carries several blooms at different stages of maturity, with flowers dropping at one end and buds opening at the other. Daylilies, wonderful in informal bouquets, are an example of this kind of flower; each blossom lasts only a day but is replaced by other blooms opening on the same stem. (Pluck spent

Flowers gathered from the garden should be brought immediately into a cool place, away from the sun, to be conditioned. After the lower foliage has been removed, the stems should be recut under water in the conditioning container and allowed to stand for several hours until stems are turgid and flowers crisp. The addition of sugar or a floral preservative to the conditioning water will prolong vase life.

blossoms daily to keep the bouquet fresh-looking.) Although criteria for defining freshness blur, it is safe to say that when the flowers cease to delight, the limit has been reached.

Cutting Flowers

Happily for most gardeners, most healthy cut flowers will keep reasonably well in a vase if tendered a little basic attention beforehand. Begin by cutting them when their stems and leaves are full of water—in either early morning or early evening. During the middle of a sunny day, moisture evaporates faster than it can be replenished, and flowers picked then are prone to wilt. Pick anytime on an overcast day. If it is more convenient to arrange flowers in the evening,

pick early in the day; the flowers can be left to condition in a pail of water and will be ready by evening. If you like to fix flowers in the morning, cut them late the day before and condition them overnight. Flowers gathered late in the day will have stored nutrients during the day and thus be in prime condition.

Take a pail of water (one-third full is adequate; more is better if you can manage it) to the garden and place the flowers in it as you cut. If this is not practical, carry a shallow, flat-bottomed basket lined with wet newspapers and lay the blossoms between the sheets with the heads hanging over the edge, taking care they do not touch the soil. Cut quickly and do not allow the basket or pail to stay long in the sun. Shorter-stemmed flowers—pansies, agera-tums, petunias—which are hard to handle, can be kept together in separate bunches with rubber bands or twist ties; this will save you the task of sorting them later.

Use sharp clippers or scissors for cutting stems and foliage; if they are dull, they can damage the water-conducting tubes in the stems. Cut only fresh flowers and bypass any that are damaged by insects or disease. Buds that show color will continue to develop after being cut, and in general, flowers are best picked just before they open. Some exceptions are irises, peonies, and roses, which last longer if cut when less than half open; zinnias, marigolds, daisies, and chrysanthemums are best cut in full bloom, but while their centers are still firm and green. Skip blooms that are dusted with pollen; they are past their prime.

Optimum times differ for cutting flowers that bloom progressively in clusters, or in florets, on a stem—lilacs, lilies, hydrangeas, and delphiniums, for example. While guidelines are given in individual Plant Profiles and you can experiment with others, in general, wait until lowest buds are fully open and upper buds are on the threshold. When cutting tulips and daffodils, leave some foliage behind on the plant to manufacture food so the bulb can build up its strength for the following year. For the same reason, never cut more than about one-half of the leaves on a flowering stem of lilies. The optimum time for cut-ting ornamental grasses is just after they bloom. I cut them when they reach the desired color or when I want them.

Conditioning

Flowers can be conditioned in various ways, and many experiments have been done in an effort to accommodate those with eccentricities. Experts use their own bag of tricks, born of experience, but it is baffling to find no consensus about the longevity of certain plants, no matter how they are conditioned. Perhaps the secret to success depends in part on the particular cultivar one works with.

The flowers of the majority of plants respond well to a simple conditioning regimen. Immediately on returning to the house with your cut flowers, strip from the stems any foliage that will fall below the waterline in both the conditioning container and in the vase; leaves decay rapidly in water, creating a haven for

Well-conditioned healthy flowers such as those shown on the facing page need little arranging to make an appealing bouquet. Pink dahlias, rosy Sedum 'Autumn Joy', and carmine snapdragons blend with light pink asters and mauve globe amaranth in a casual arrangement that reflects the late summer garden.

bacteria. Spare some top foliage if you want it for decoration, but because water evaporates through the leaves, it is good practice to reduce their number. (On the other hand, chrysanthemums and pansies last longer if their foliage is left on.) With a sharp knife, recut the stems at an angle and plunge them into a bucket of warm water, submerging about three-quarters of their length. Warm water is absorbed faster than cold, but the temperature should be no higher than 100°F; hot water can cook the stems, especially the more delicate ones. Use only fresh water and spanking clean containers. Allow the flowers to stand in the water as it cools. If they are to be arranged in a vase of water, a few hours is ample; if they are to be inserted in floral foam let them stand in water overnight (or at least eight hours). Treat flowering plumes of ornamental grasses the same way. To keep the stems of tulips straight, or to support tall stems, wrap newspapers around them, including the heads, before standing them in water.

Greenery is especially easy to condition, and foliage from galax, pachysandra, euonymus, ivy, and other ground covers and vines is remarkably long lasting. Submerge mature leaves in cold water for about an hour, or until crisp; young, tender leaves need less time. If you do not intend to use the foliage soon, it will keep almost forever stored in a plastic bag in the refrigerator.

Certain plants require an extra step. The cut stems of poppies, holly-

hocks, hibiscus, and oleander, for instance, ooze a milky or yellowish latex. If the ends of the stems are untreated, this sap will coagulate and clog the stem's water-conducting tubes. To prevent this, make a few slits in the stem end and sear it for about half a minute over a candle or gas flame, or dip it into a few inches of boiling water for about a minute. Take care to apply heat only briefly lest too many of the water-conducting cells be damaged in the process. Protect the flower petals from rising steam either by holding the flower heads out of the steam or by putting a newspaper collar around the flower heads. Finish conditioning in a deep, water-filled container.

Plants with hollow stems generally last well when conditioned in warm water, but if you want maximum longevity, turn your daffodils or dahlias or other hollow-stemmed flowers upside down after they are conditioned, fill the cavities with water, and plug with cotton. (Or insert chenille pipe

ABOVE *Handfuls of short-stemmed pansies crowded into hidden jars of water create a cheerful spring garden inside a wooden box. Pansy flowers are best appreciated when their faces are turned toward the viewer.*

FACING PAGE *Conditioning of cut material varies with the plant and how it is to be used.* Salvia farinacea *'Victoria' should be allowed a long drink in warm water before being arranged with other flowers. After it has been immersed in cold water until crisp, the ivy foliage can be held in a plastic bag in the refrigerator for future use. The foxtail grass, perfect for a winter bouquet, should be dried standing upright in a container with a few inches of water.*

PAGES 124–125 *Annuals and light picking from the author's cutting garden provide the basis for many bouquets. Pails on the bench hold red dahlias, mauve* Salvia viridis *'Claryssa', and clear pink lavatera. Assorted containers on the brick terrace hold apple green bells-of-Ireland, two crimson swags of love-lies-bleeding, zinnias, orange tithonia, marigolds, sunflowers, and a giant amber bloom of an old dahlia.*

with a mallet for better water absorption, rinse off any bits of stem, then condition in warm water. Heavy woody stems of shrubs and trees also benefit from being dunked in several inches of water at 100–120°F for a few minutes before the container is filled with warm water. A teaspoon of laundry bleach added to each quart of water in the vase will control bacteria and keep the water sweet.

Flowers such as roses, snapdragons, carnations, annual chrysanthemums, and asters benefit by having their stems cut under water to prevent air bubbles from forming in stem tissue and impeding water uptake. (Japanese arrangers cut all flowers under water.) Condition them in the same water in which they are cut; if the stems are exposed to air at any time, they should be recut under water. Some plants display other idiosyncrasies, and these are mentioned where they apply in the Plant Profiles and the list of Annuals in the Appendix. Learning what they are will make it easier for you to respond beneficially.

Whatever the flower, nothing can substitute for tender loving care—careful cutting and conditioning and practicing good plant hygiene.

For many of us, nevertheless, the transient nature of a beautiful bouquet is part of its fascination, and brings the same keen pleasure as the short-lived happiness that comes from writing in the sand at the beach, knowing that all will vanish with the tide.

A formal airy arrangement in a tole planter uses a restricted color range and fluffy flower heads of hydrangeas, the meadowsweet Filipendula palmata *'Nana', and smokebush (*Cotinus coggygria*); foxglove* Digitalis purpurea *'Alba' lends vertical line.*

cleaners, which will wick up water and keep the stem firm and flexible.) I confess that I have never gone this extra mile, but some experts insist such pampering will add many hours to the life of these flowers.

Branches of trees, shrubs, and certain other woody-stemmed plants such as perennial chrysanthemums and some artemisias also need special treatment. Make two or three vertical slits a few inches long at the base of their stems or crush the stem ends

Flower Arranging

Flower arranging is a joyful experience open to nearly everyone. Despite the evanescence of the live flowers that are its materials, it is an art form that has been around since before the birth of Christ. Flower arrangements are displayed on Egyptian tombs, Roman frescoes, Persian carpets, and many other antiquities. The practice has spanned centuries, outlived civilizations, leapt over oceans, and is alive and well today.

Countless of its practitioners have been held in thrall, and this addiction comes in several guises. There are those in the grip of re-creating period designs such as French rococo, Victorian, Art Deco, or Colonial American. There are those happy bands of garden-club arrangers who compete in flower shows. A distinguished minority are drawn to variations of the Japanese classic ikebana style, which in its purest form is a spiritual discipline as well as high art. But informal, personal arrangements created with gorgeous flowers grown in one's own garden are second to none in the pleasure they give.

It's said that flowers are so beautiful in themselves that it's hard to make them look ugly. Indeed, haphazard bouquets of fresh garden flowers can be irresistible; they have their time and place and are easy to arrange. All through the growing season, you can have weekly bowls or pitchers with samples of all the colorful and fragrant flowers that bloom in your garden, casually placed

to radiate their charm in the rooms where you spend the most time.

You might wish to fill a supporting cast of mugs, tankards, and bud vases with seasonal handfuls of scillas, violas, sweet peas, nasturtiums, nepetas, ageratums, nigellas, mignonettes, and sprigs of herbs—perhaps mint, parsley, basil, and rosemary. These will brighten a kitchen windowsill, writing desk, nightstand, bathroom vanity, bookshelves. Meals at the kitchen table can be enhanced

Spring branches and flowers were gleaned from gardens of family and friends by the groom's mother to make these captivating arrangements for a June wedding reception. Lovely flowering dogwood branches give structure to the large arrangement, and the classic floral motif of peonies, iris, tulips, and lilacs is repeated in a charming ivy-covered wire basket on the table.

ABOVE *An effervescent bouquet in a nineteenth-century English pitcher captures the informality of this comfortable setting. The flowers are both garden and roadside varieties, including Queen-Anne's-lace, Joe-Pye weed, coneflowers, roses, perennial sweet pea, and the tiny lavender flowers of oregano.*

FACING PAGE *A simple but generous bunch of Sensation cosmos becomes the perfect accompaniment to a blue-and-white spatterware pitcher with a hollyberry motif. Flowers grown for cutting in the owners' garden are selected in forms and colors that will combine well with their extensive collection of early English and American ceramics.*

by a simple bean pot flaunting the flowers of the day—golden coreopsis, creamy zinnias, blue salvia, lime lady's-mantle. A perfect bloom of the most sumptuous flower in your garden—tree peony, lily, dahlia—can float in a shallow crystal dish in the dining room. At times, all that is needed is a single beautiful flower in a simple container.

Bouquets can be cut and fashioned in hand as you stroll the garden in the early morning or evening. Strip off the lower leaves immediately and throw them on the compost pile. Rotate the bunch as you add stems to balance the bouquet, then cut them all to the same length. It takes but a few minutes more to slip the flowers into containers filled

with tepid water and set them where they will be most enjoyed. (And since there are plenty more where they came from, you needn't be scrupulous about conditioning them.)

Such arranging requires no fussing about where each stem or bunch should go. It's an easy, comfortable ritual and gives so much in return—color, vitality, a sense of well-being.

For those times when more ambitious arrangements are called for, however, allow yourself to exercise that creative impulse that lurks in the heart of each of us. The often intimidating rules of traditional arranging styles involving line, line-mass, open triangle, right-angle triangle, symmetrical triangle, asymmetrical triangle, diagonal, Hogarth curve,

Spry set out to "debunk the idea that there are certain set rules of right and wrong for the arrangement of flowers." She was a master of detail, line, color blending, and satisfying balance, but she also encouraged each individual to "work to the pattern of his own ideas," lest there be an end of originality. Add to this the availability of an ever-increasing range of plants to grow and work with. In all, there has never been a more agreeable time to take up arranging flowers, especially for those who have taken the trouble to grow their own.

You can begin a bouquet from different points of view. Gardeners are prone to cut whatever flowers the garden offers, arrange them in a container, and then look around for a place to put them where they will contribute most to a room. Another approach is to begin with a favorite vase and choose the flowers and setting to go with it. You might want flowers for a special occasion, or for a particular place in a room—a dresser in a blue-and-white guest room or a table on a stair landing.

There is no arguing that it will make life simpler if you have an idea of what you want, where you will put it, and what you have to work with. These are fairly practical matters, and for the most part, common sense will guide you. An arrangement intended to be placed against a wall or other flat surface can be flat on one side (avoid making a flat fan shape of it; positioning some of the blooms forward for a three-dimensional effect is much more attractive), while

Flowers make dining more festive, whether indoors or on the patio in summer. These floribunda and hybrid tea roses from a cutting garden, casually placed in water in a few tankards and a spongeware beanpot that pick up the colors of the plates, need no arranging.

spiral, and other geometric forms do not necessarily have to be followed. Nor do the mysteries of composition, converging and diverging lines, symmetry, and balance need to be fully understood to make pleasing "sophisticated" arrangements. There are many ways to proceed.

A liberating trend away from the neat, almost painfully balanced arrangements of the past toward today's free-flowing designs began in the 1930s when England's Constance

flowers on a coffee table will be viewed from above, or from all sides, like a sculpture. If it is important to have a bouquet relate to a room's decor, either to the whole picture or to a small area within the room, be sure to weigh colors, textures, and designs for mutual enhancement. Each time flowers are brought into a room, they will refresh it, bringing new colors, textures, and moods.

CONTAINERS

Containers are an integral part of the flower arrangement and should be chosen carefully. Those in plain shapes and neutral colors are the most versatile. They allow attention to focus on the flowers and will work with any style of decor. A container with a busy pattern or brilliant colors presents a challenge, as it might dominate the arrangement. One way to handle this situation is to place the flowers in a dramatic or a boldly simple arrangement (simplicity itself is often dramatic).

Containers come in so many sizes, shapes, textures, colors, and materials it is hard to winnow the choices for a good basic collection. Storage space may be the limiting factor. Often, it's wisest to select a few basic shapes that appeal to you and look well in your home; you can always vary the arrangements you make in them.

Containers need not be costly. Scour flea markets, craft shows,

The informality and classic charm of zinnias are enhanced by the yellowware jugs used as containers and placed about on a breakfast buffet table. Keeping the flowers in separate-color bouquets instead of one large mixed arrangement results in a most appealing display. When the foliage is in good shape and left on the stems above the water line, it provides a fine background for showing off the flowers. Seen here are lime-green Envy, red Purple Prince, orange California State, and rose-pink scabiosa-flowered zinnias.

gift shops, garage sales, department stores, and antique shops. The search itself can be a pleasant hobby.

Your home, however, probably is already full of containers that can be used to hold flowers even if they were originally intended for another purpose. Water and wine glasses and goblets, baking dishes and molds, jam jars and sugar bowls, wine carafes and soup tureens can become appealing (and unusual) receptacles. Miniature bottles, flasks, and antique inkwells make wonderful bud vases. Favorite baskets or wooden boxes that are visually appealing but not watertight can be fitted with inexpensive plastic liners (even plastic freezer containers) to hold water. Attractive bouquets can be made in a tumbler or jar set inside the container and the flowers allowed to cascade over the sides as camouflage. This is a good technique for

TOP *Twin vases of pink and red old roses arranged with lady's-mantle (*Alchemilla mollis*) brighten the sideboard and play on the shapes in the painting above.*

BOTTOM *A whimsical arrangement of sparkling red hollyhocks, white false dragonhead (*Physostegia virginiana*) and* Artemisia ludoviciana *'Silver King' is placed among curios.*

FACING PAGE *The classic pedestal and urn demand a large, bold arrangement, which is accomplished in a Victorian mood. Among the flowers are intricately patterned sweet William; red, white, and pink astilbe; verbascum; pink mallow (*Malva alcea *'Fastigiata'); lupine; and plumy smokebush.*

utilizing wide-mouthed containers when no floral foam or pinholder is at hand.

A container with a narrow neck is the easiest to work with because it offers good support for the stems. The clean, eloquent shape of the classic Oriental ginger jar is a joy to work with. Glass fishbowls and other globe shapes, such as giant brandy snifters, also make good containers for showing off handsome stems such as those of tulips, daffodils, and hyacinths. Cylinders can make some flowers stand up and salute; those with long, supple stems give in to gravity by bowing gracefully. Trumpet-shaped vases allow stems to bend naturally, but the bouquets they hold will often benefit when a mechanical aid or a

KNOWING YOUR FLOWERS

Inspiration will come from the flowers themselves. While growing and nurturing your own flowers, you will have gained valuable insights about their forms, colors, and habits. This sensitivity will be a great help in placing them to best advantage in a vase. With experience, just looking at a cut flower stem will tell you how and where to put it.

Daffodils, stocks, snapdragons, delphiniums, and lilies, to name a few, have relatively straight stems and can provide a good background structure or outline for an arrangement; hellebores, poppies, coreopsis, cosmos, shasta daisies, nicotiana, clematis, Japanese anemone, and myriad more gently nod, curve, or trail, imparting grace and softness. Tulips are among the most fascinating dynamic single element in a bouquet; they will curve, stretch, grow, open, close, and turn toward the light, and can be reshuffled and recut to maintain scale and balance.

Some flowers are of bold, aristocratic character, the showpieces in the garden and in an arrangement; others are dainty, less assertive, congenial performers content to grow quietly—among them baby's-breath, alyssum, *Coreopsis verticillata* 'Moonbeam', calamint (*Calamintha nepeta*)—making them good "fillers" for your bouquets. You will be able to pick selectively for the effect you want.

STYLES OF ARRANGING

Simple but beautiful arrangements can be made with only a few flowers,

cage fashioned of crossed stems or branches is used to hold stems toward the center. Cubes, rectangles, and low, open-mouthed bowls usually require floral foam, chicken wire, pinholders, or their like to support stems.

ABOVE *A small, artistically pleasing arrangement is created with strong rounded shapes in a rounded container. The off-center focal point, a startling white columbine, is balanced by a purple spike of* Salvia farinacea *and purple fountain grass.*

BELOW *The strong sculptural simplicity of the white pitcher requires an assertive arrangement for a dramatic effect, which is fulfilled by bold orange tulips.*

LEFT *An inexpensive blue-and-white vase carries a creative traditional arrangement with all the grace of a priceless antique. Roses, airy sprays of white cosmos and phlox, and spiky lines of iris foliage and pink larkspur stand out against a plain neutral background.*

ABOVE *A lively centerpiece in a silver bowl completes the table setting in an elegant dining room. Evergreen, shade-loving Christmas fern (* Polystichum acrostichoides) *covers the floral foam with its greenery.*

FACING PAGE *A large arrangement on a contemporary glass coffee table, viewable from all sides, seems to be suspended in air. Such a well-built arrangement, in soft classic colors and a clear glass container, lends its charm to many settings without detracting from background patterns and works of art. The arrangement here uses spiky white gladioluses and delphinium, round focal points of rubrum lilies and* Phlox paniculata *'Bright Eyes', and tiny, buttonlike flowers of the yarrow* Achillea ptarmica *'Angel's Breath' as filler.*

requiring few decisions. More intricate bouquets with many different flowers require more complex judgments. You can work with a style that is luxuriant and assertive or one that is light and airy. The first approach is a wonderful way to show off the exuberance of the summer garden. It requires a bounty of sumptuous flowers, mostly large-flowered perennials such as phlox, hydrangea, and delphinium, annuals of substance such as sunflowers and African marigolds, and craggy branches. The container should be crammed artfully with as many stems as it will hold to simulate an exuberant hodgepodge.

The latter style is lighter and uses smaller, more delicate flowers, perhaps sweet peas, cosmos, nicotiana, Iceland poppies, nigella, trailing nasturtiums, and cup-and-saucer vine (*Cobaea scandens*), airy grasses, and gentler perennials such as Russian sage, campanula, and veronica. Framed by open spaces, some blooms will stand out powerfully. Other blossoms, recessed inside the bouquet and on another plane, will reveal themselves subtly. With a stem or two of Japanese anemone floating above and a small-flowered species clematis curling below, such bouquets can be achingly lovely.

One or the other of these two major styles may be more expressive of your personality, but be adventurous and try both. It's fun, and it widens your options to be able to switch back and forth depending on the occasion, setting, your mood, and the flowers you have to work with.

TECHNIQUE

There are many facets to arranging and room for much diversity in viewpoint and technique. No one book could exhaust them all. The following ideas have been helpful to me. Perhaps they will motivate you to try your hand or provide a few new ideas if you are already addicted.

Flower arranging follows general guidelines, both practical and aesthetic. The artistic principles are more general, personal, and elusive and apply to all artistic compositions. They involve concepts of balance, harmony, color quality, texture, and form. Every time a stem is positioned in an arrangement, these concepts are being juggled, even if subconsciously. You will become acutely aware when something seems out of kilter and will adjust it until you are satisfied. Seemingly intuitive judgments about what works best are based on observation and learning and come with experience. How these concepts are individually interpreted is what gives each bouquet its special punch.

Assemble your flowers and container and put in place any chicken wire, floral foam, or pinholder you may be using to support the flowers. Conceal this base with foliage or moss so that it will not detract from the finished arrrangement. These supportive underpinnings, or "mechanics," are discussed more fully on pages 145 and 146.

Position two or three of the sturdiest, most important branches or

*The classic beauty of pink Sarah Bernhardt peonies, Siberian irises, clematis, and foxgloves (*Digitalis ambigua*) in a blue transfer ware pitcher enhance a traditional setting.*

A creative display of roses brings a touch of magic to a formal living room. A tall vase is floral designer Pauline Runkle's favorite container for arranging long canes of English roses from her garden. A secondary bouquet around the base provides stability and added beauty.

stems on opposite sides of the container so they reach out to the sides to establish the width of the arrangement; then insert a stem of the tallest flowers to determine the height. Try not to place it dead center: this can result in a stiff triangular structure. Also avoid the "rabbit's ears" silhouette. A lopsided arrangement can easily result if you go too far in one direction and a stiff one if you overcompensate for lopsidedness. Beware of both pitfalls. If you are in doubt about how high to make the design, a common rule of thumb for a pleasing scale is to keep the flowers to two-and-a-half times the height of the container. With this basic structure in place, you are now ready to proceed.

Add your other flowers, placing them in pleasing relationship to each other and to the container. In a mixed bouquet, work with one kind of flower at a time until they are all used up, beginning with the more important heavier flowers and ending with the lighter, fluffier blossoms, which you can use as fillers to weave the bouquet together. (Try baby's-breath or, even better, sea lavender or a couple of stems of the classy chartreuse *Bupleurum rotundifolium*, a hardy annual.) Save your star performers, a red dahlia, for example, or orange Enchantment lilies (still my favorite for garden and vase) that will create the focal point, until last so you can place them for maximum effect. If the bouquet is to be seen from all sides,

keep turning it as you work to examine it from different vantage points and to keep it from becoming lopsided. Keep color in mind, blending or contrasting as you prefer.

When the bouquet is finished, note whether the mechanics are completely concealed; if not, add more leafy camouflage. Stand back and evaluate it from different angles. If the balance is off, try removing a stem in the problem area, or reset the angle, or insert a bloom with the desired visual weight. Make adjustments until you are satisfied, and then place it where you can enjoy it.

SPECIAL TIPS

It's the extra care and little touches that can make your bouquet more pleasing and personal, that will set it apart from a mass-produced commercial bouquet or centerpiece. Consider the following:

Insert each stem at the same angle toward an imaginary focal point. This will strengthen the unity of the bouquet and make it appear more natural, as if the flowers are all growing from the same main root.

Dotting flowers around the arrangement, one here matched by its twin on the other side, for a perfect balance can create a boring arrangement. Asymmetrical balance will give a more interesting and natural look to your bouquets. Balance two small flowers, say roses, on one side by a larger rose or a single multiflowered stem of feverfew on the other. Each

BELOW *A Loetz iridescent glass vase holds an extraordinary artistic arrangement, which is part of a larger composition including Art Nouveau glass objects and a painting in the background. The motif of the gold fabric, designed and dyed by the arranger, was inspired by the spiky racemes of cimicifuga growing in the garden and also used in the arrangement. Among other flowers, foliage, and seedpods used here are sweet pepperbush* (Clethra alnifolia), *smokebush, oak-leaved hydrangea, various twining clematis and sweet peas, dill, parsley, bupleurum, nigella, and meadow rue* (Thalictrum sp.).

FACING PAGE *A galvanized conditioning can doubles as a vase for a casual arrangement of bold hydrangeas, agapanthus, and yellow lilies.*

time you add a stem, it will disrupt or adjust the balance. If you feel that you are constantly correcting as you go along, you're on the right track.

Turn some flowers in the bouquet so that they "talk to" each other, rather than face them all outward; this will encourage the viewer to eavesdrop. Use different heights to lend an in-and-out rhythm to the bouquet, which is more appealing than a static creation on a single plane.

Foliage is important; it should complement the blooms. For example, magnolia or rhododendron leaves would look silly in a bouquet of fragile, delicately colored blooms, but hosta leaves meet their match with peonies. The most pleasing

natural look results when only foliage from the flowers in the bouquet is used. Save some of the leaves that you remove from the stems during conditioning to be used as extra greenery, especially the more attractive, longer-lasting kinds such as rose and chrysanthemum leaves.

For a centerpiece that is made in a shallow dish, clever use of greenery is required to conceal the mechanics. If leaves other than those on the flowers in the arrangement are used, try mixing different kinds, European ginger and trailing ivy, for instance, or sprigs of herbs (parsley and basil), or pieris, mahonia, leucothoe, and periwinkle. Instead of covering the mechanics first with greenery, or making a ruff around the bowl in the

traditional way, use foliage sparingly, anticipating that stems used in the arrangement will partially conceal it. Extra leaves or moss can be tucked nimbly in at the end. As for height, a centerpiece that is no taller than about a foot will keep the view across the table clear. Professional floral designers say that the most comfortable average line of sight across the dining table is between 11 and 15 inches.

At first, you may feel timid, but with experience the logic that guides the sequence will become spontaneous and you will soon be creating beautiful bouquets with ease. Above all, make a bouquet that delights you; it cannot help but bring pleasure to others.

AFTER-CARE

Continuing to care for the flowers after they are arranged can prolong the life of a bouquet. Unless you can do so easily and without disrupting the arrangement, it's not necessary to replace the water in the container. But it is important to keep the water level topped off in the vase or liner holding the floral foam. Check water level every day.

Remove faded blossoms regularly and recut stems. Recutting stems of some flowers will lengthen their life and encourage more florets to open; some of the flowers that benefit from this procedure are foxgloves, delphiniums, scabiosas, mums, daisies, snapdragons, roses, and agapanthus. If they flag prematurely, some roses, violets, and hydrangeas will perk up after being submerged in tepid water for an hour or two. If stems of rudbeckia or shasta daisies go limp, often they can be revived by recutting them, wrapping them in

LEFT *Yarrow and feverfew (*Tanacetum parthenium*) are wonderful reliable partners for long-lasting country bunches as they always seem to be in bloom. Here they are used as the basis for a cheerful yellow-and-white arrangement, with greenery and a few spiky white flowers—delphinium, foxglove, and astilbe—poked in among them.*

FACING PAGE *Roses, yarrow, Zinnia 'Dreamland Salmon', agapanthus, and red-hot-poker are some of the flowers in a compact, late summer arrangement that brightens a corner of a terrace in Woodside, California. A rustic container lends a country flavor, but the arrangement would look equally at home indoors in a copper or brass holder, or in a porcelain bowl.*

newspaper, and standing them in a bucket of warm water for a few hours.

Keep the bouquet out of strong sunlight and move it to a cool place at night and during the times you are not there to enjoy it. Remember to readjust the bouquet after discarding dead flowers. After recutting stems a few times, you might want to rearrange them in a smaller container.

A few drops of laundry bleach or ammonia will keep the water clear (no more than a teaspoon to a quart of water); commercial florists do this to deter bacterial growth. Aspirin, which is acidic, is also effective. A lump of washed activated charcoal added to the water will absorb products of decay and offensive odors.

Commercial floral preservatives are available at flower shops and hardware stores. Many contain silver nitrate, which delays aging in flowers but may react chemically with metal containers and weaken the effectiveness of the preservatives. A pinch of sugar might help, since plants need sugar to carry on metabolic proc-

esses. Pennies, despite the folklore, are useless as a floral preservative. I have it on good authority that alcohol, scotch, bourbon, sake, or whatever is close at hand, works wonders for keeping grasses, reeds, and bamboos lively; the English claim that a splash of champagne revives wilting clematis as nothing else will.

After the bouquet is discarded, scrub the container with hot soapy water and a little bleach.

TOOLS AND EQUIPMENT

Space is at a premium in many homes today, but try to set aside a small area where you can keep standby containers and arrange flowers. Perhaps space (ideally close to a water source) can be found on a side porch, or in the laundry room or garage. At least keep in a separate basket or box, which you can bring out at a moment's notice, the few tools and mechanical aids that you will use most often. Having the right tools and aids close at hand will increase the pleasure of arranging and keep

the kitchen paring knives and scissors where they belong.

Nothing exotic or expensive is needed: a small, sharp knife for cutting flower stems and removing rose thorns; a pair of sharp scissors for many uses; a good pair of pruning shears (borrow these and loppers

from the garden shed) for cutting woody branches; a mallet or heavy weight for crushing woody stems. Add heavy gloves and wire cutters for cutting chicken wire and florist's tape and clay for securing mechanics to the container.

You will not need mechanics for all arrangements. Often in making a bouquet in a tallish container, twiggy branches and sturdy flower and foliage stems can be crossed below water level (at a stable, low center of gravity) into a self-supporting net for inserting other smaller stems. This will work nicely for many natural-looking

ABOVE *Cut flowers are brought indoors for various reasons—as room decor, to reflect nature and the seasons, for their beauty— but whatever the motivation, a few flowers placed strategically about a room give it an inhabited look even when nobody is there.*

FACING PAGE *A neutral container and only two kinds of flowers are used in an open, homey bouquet that brings warmth to the hearth and white brick background.*

ABOVE *Spring is symbolized in an elegant freestyle version of a Japanese Bunjin arrangement, seen in a modern room setting with an uncluttered background. Bamboo canes, clematis, and delicate maidenhair fern are combined in a small Chinese bronze vase. Japanese arrangements are traditionally displayed against a plain screen to emphasize their beauty and purity of line.*

FACING PAGE *A tantalizing floral chandelier of roses, lady's-mantle, and small foxgloves with hosta and various other foliage hangs from the ceiling inside a garden teahouse. The arrangement is made by inserting flower and foliage stems into floral foam packed in an open plastic cage. The floral foam must be kept wet.*

arrangements with garden flowers and branches, but keeping a few mechanics on hand and learning how to use them will increase the design possibilities for your arrangements, especially when you want a little more formality.

Chicken wire is the most useful prop for holding stems in large, wide-mouthed bowls and jugs. A piece about four feet square from a garden or farm supply store will serve for many arrangements. Cut it into a few smaller sheets of manageable size and loosely crumple them and press into the bowl so that they fit against the sides of the container. Sometimes simply making a grid across the mouth of the container with floral tape will provide sufficient support for stems that are then inserted between the spaces. Floral tape will not stick to a wet surface, so make sure that it, the container, and your hands are dry when applying it.

Pinholders, used extensively for Japanese and modern arrangements, are good for making arrangements in shallow dishes when a limited number of flowers will be used. They come in various sizes and shapes and sit unobtrusively on the bottom of containers, requiring little if any leaf cover-up. They hold stems securely, though somewhat rigidly, so are best suited for slender or supple-stemmed flowers that curve naturally. Floral clay can be applied to the bottom of the pinholder to affix it to the container and add more stability to the arrangement. Do this before adding water to the bowl; like floral tape,

the clay will not stick to a wet surface. Pinholders can also be used in conjunction with chicken wire to provide more support for branches in large arrangements.

Floral foam such as Oasis is easy to work with and widely used. It comes in "bricks" that can be cut to fit any container. It should be soaked in water before using. Enthusiastic arrangers often keep a moistened brick in a plastic bag in the refrigerator ready to be called into service. Floral foam comes in two forms, one that can support woody and large stems and a second suitable for smaller or softer stems.

Before beginning an arrangement, cut the foam (a kitchen knife will do) to fit the container, but so that it protrudes an inch or two above the edge. This allows some of the outside stems to be positioned almost horizontally into the foam to establish the silhouette of the arrangement. Other flowers can trail gracefully over the sides of the container. Two strips of floral tape across the top of the foam will hold it in the container. Conceal the top of the foam with foliage, flowers, or moss.

Pebbles, marbles, polished stones, and sand can be used to anchor stems in arrangements, and these can look attractive in glass containers. Use them carefully, to avoid damaging delicate stems. Place them in the container first, then add the stems.

Most of the mechanics you will need are readily available at hardware and variety stores or at florists and floral supply shops.

FLOWERS
IN WINTER

And so the ripe year wanes. From turfy slopes afar the breeze brings
delicious, pungent, spicy odors from the wild Everlasting flowers. . . .
I gather the seed-pods in the garden beds, sharing their bounty with
the birds I love so well, for there are enough and to spare for us all.
—Celia Thaxter
An Island Garden, 1894

ABOVE *The floral motif of the porcelain vase could well have been the inspiration for this glowing massed arrangement of roses, larkspur, foxglove, zinnias, tansy, tulips, and narcissus.*

FACING PAGE *Masses of roses in an antique porcelain footed bowl suit the Victorian decor of the New York City apartment of Jeanne Chappell, an arranger of dried flowers. Dried hydrangea foliage fills in around the roses, and celosia is mixed with red roses in the two smaller classic urns flanking the bowl.*

PAGES 148–149 *Diverse makings for dried arrangements include cockscomb, hydrangea, seedpods of false indigo (*Baptisia austra-lis*), nandina berries, and dried okra, a vegetable.*

PAGE 149 *Ivy leaves dried in sand and fashioned into a wreath, attractive as is, can be decorated with dried herbs and flowers.*

Dried flowers are the star performers of winter arrangements—especially everlastings, those flowers with papery petals that air-dry well. In parts of the country where winters are bleak, a store of dried flowers, foliage, and seedpods, picked in their prime during the growing season, can be immensely useful. A cheerful basket of bright everlastings in the family room or a more formal arrangement of dried roses, peonies, and delphiniums in a cherished Delft bowl in the entrance hall will more than return the foresight and effort that went into creating it. Growing, drying, and arranging flowers for such bouquets is yet another engrossing byway of gardening.

Drying flowers has a less obvious advantage that only gardeners can appreciate. Sometimes, we go into the garden to cut flowers and find a bloom that is so stunning, so indescribably perfect in color or shape, we wish we could keep it forever just as it is. While all cut plant materials have a limited life-span, drying them allows us to savor their beauty over a long period. How long depends on how well we protect them from strong light and humidity—the two culprits that will undo them.

Dried flower arrangements—those that are in impeccable condition and carefully designed—are much more than mere substitutes for fresh bunches. Each has its place. Obviously, dried flowers cannot exude the same vitality that living flowers do, but their rich textures and colors are far more complex than is generally appreciated. A dried bouquet can encompass the harvest of all the seasons at once. It can include spring's columbines, pansies, daffodils, and tulips; summer's roses, delphiniums, and a host of others; and the hydrangeas, fiery foliage, seedpods, and architectural branches of fall and winter. Colors can range from subtle to dramatic, as some flowers keep their clear, bright hues during the drying process while others become muted. Textures and shapes will vary from supple to crisp or brittle. A good percentage of the flowers will look realistic; a few will have undergone a metamorphosis, as if touched by a fairy's wand—red roses turned to burgundy black.

Unless you are just starting a garden, you probably already grow many of the plants that can be dried successfully. If you have a mixed border from which you can gather perennials, annuals, flowering shrubs, and roses, this should furnish you with a good and varied selection. Collect enough flowers throughout the growing season to provide you with two or three winter arrangements, but pick and dry at least twice the supply you think you will need, to make up for shrinkage dur-

ing drying and the shattering that will occur no matter how carefully you work with them.

Many of the stalwarts of the cutting garden for fresh bouquets are equally good as dried flowers. A few of the more useful ones are snapdragons (Rocket and the Butterfly series), *Salvia farinacea* 'Blue Bedder', cockscombs (*Celosia* spp.), amaranths, zinnias, and cosmos. If you have space in the cutting garden or vegetable plot, a few rows could be given over to everlastings, which look much

ABOVE *Flowers and foliage in many sizes, shapes, and colors should be picked and dried throughout the growing season. Flowers and stems should be crisp and turgid when picked to hold the best form while drying. If plants are wilted, condition them in deep water first; this does not affect drying time or color retention.*

BELOW *Berries and grasses may be picked at different stages and air-dried either by hanging them upside down or standing their stems upright in a container in a warm dry place.*

FACING PAGE *This warm-toned arrangement, made by George von Tobel, a floral designer in Greenwich, Connecticut, uses yarrow, celosia, scabiosa, hydrangea, blue larkspur, and berried eucalyptus leaves.*

the same whether fresh or dried.
They include the ever-popular strawflowers (*Helichrysum bracteatum*) and
annual statice (*Limonium sinuatum*),
which come in a striking array of colors. Other classic annuals for drying
are *Acroclinium roseum,* globe amaranth
(*Gomphrena globosa*), love-in-a-mist
(*Nigella damascena*), and drumstick
scabious (*Scabiosa stellata*). Surpris-
ingly, zinnias do not air-dry well and
require the use of a drying agent.

Ornamental grasses of all kinds
impart a lively airiness to dried
arrangements, whether from their
dried foliage, flowering plumes, or
seed panicles. A few annual grasses
that are staples among a score of
others for drying are the big and little quaking grasses (*Briza maxima* and
B. minor), with their curious woven
spikelets that quiver in the air; hare's-
tail grass (*Lagurus ovatus*), squirreltail
grass (*Hordeum jubatum*), and foxtail
millet (*Setaria italica*). Harvesting and
drying all grasses is a simple project.
Just cut stems, tie and hang them in
a dry place, or stand them in a dry
container to bend naturally if you
want arching stems.

Scour the entire garden for drying
material to add to your cache. Shade
gardens will offer foliage and blooms
from astilbes, hostas, and hellebores.
Various hydrangeas, prized by arrangers for their versatility and range
of lovely colors, grow well in partial
shade and can be picked at any stage
after the flowers are fully opened.
Many ferns thrive in shade and can
be easily dried by pressing. Their
lacy, arched fronds are wonderful

grace notes in dried bouquets, in
which many other stems are stiff and
straight. Use them simply, interspersed with autumn leaves and
bright berries. My favorites are the
dainty Japanese painted fern (*Athyr-
ium nipponicum* 'Pictum') with silver-
splashed fronds and rosy veins, and
the more robust evergreen Christmas
fern (*Polystichum acrostichoides*).

Foliage can also be collected from
ground covers, vines, shrubs, and
trees (especially sprays of beech, maple, and poplar) and either pressed
or treated with glycerin. Autumn
foliage that has turned color generally does not take up glycerin well;
pressing gives better results.

Harvesting Flowers

When and how the flowers are harvested are as important as how they
are dried and stored. Collect plants
and dry them, a few at a time,
throughout spring, summer, and fall.
Midmorning on a sunny day after
the dew has evaporated is the best
time for picking. Generally, pick
flowers just after they have opened,
and select the most flawless blooms
you can find; drying will magnify
imperfections. But also collect a few
buds, semiopened blossoms, and
seedpods as well as full-blown specimens; they will inject a dynamic
mood into a dried arrangement that
belies its static condition.

Drying Methods and Storage

Air-drying is the easiest way to dry
a quantity of flowers at one time and
to preserve a great range of natural

colors. Some shrinkage and change of color will take place, but flowers dried in this way are charming and evoke a nostalgia for an earlier time when drying flowers, particularly herbs, was an important part of daily life. Dry a few herbs, at least sage, mint, and lavender, for flowers, foliage, and fragrance.

The more quickly a plant is dried, the better it will retain its color and shape. Find an airy, warm, dry, dimly lit place for drying; an attic is perfect. Strip all leaves from the stems, then tie small bunches of the same kind of flowers together (stagger the heads), and hang them head down by their stems from a coat hanger, hook, peg, or rack. Air circulation around each flower head is important. Drying can take from two to several weeks, depending on the size of the flowers and the humidity of the drying room.

Support large, flat blooms of Queen-Anne's-lace, yarrow, dill, and others by slipping their stems through wire screening (chicken wire will do) and let them dry right side up.

Variations on the air-drying method include standing stems (especially grasses) to dry naturally in a dry container or placing them upright in a few inches of water to dry slowly as they absorb the water. Hydrangeas dry well this way, as do some roses, alliums, heather, larkspur, and hosta leaves. The stems of material dried standing upright will curve slightly, usually a desirable outcome.

Strawflowers are the most popu-

lar for drying. Cut flower heads when the outer two to four rows of "petals" (actually bracts) are open. Leave only ½ inch of stem, and insert the end of a 21-gauge wire through the stub just into the center of the flower. Cut the wire to leave a "stem" from six to eight inches long. Stand the wired flowers in a container, or stick the wire stems into a block of Styrofoam and leave in an airy place until dry. Wrap green floral tape around the wire stems for a more natural

An exuberant interpretation of a Dutch Flemish style has been created with dried flowers in which streaked tulips, lilies, peonies, roses, hydrangea, larkspur, nigella, cockscomb, and other flowers with different blooming times are assembled in one arrangement.

look. The head will tighten around the wire as it dries, and the flower will open fully.

Carefully store the dried material in boxes between layers of tissue paper. Place a few mothballs in the box to deter rodents and insects, and label the boxes to avoid confusion later. Flowers that have been hung to dry can be left hanging, and those dried in upright containers can be left in place in a dry atmosphere away from sunlight and damaging dust or dirt.

Drying agents such as silica gel, borax, cornmeal, and alum will extend the range of plants that can be dried with good results. Sand drying also works well; unlike the drying agents or desiccants mentioned, which absorb moisture from plant tissue, sand simply supports flowers while they dry naturally. Unlike in the air-drying method, only a few flowers can be dried at a time, depending on how much of the drying substance is on hand.

The desiccant silica gel is the fastest and most popular medium for drying individual flowers. Use it for "problem" flowers—tulips, daffodils, peonies, and other large blooms. Because flowers in silica gel dry so quickly, their colors remain clear and bright and their textures and shapes lifelike, but they become very brittle, and strict timing is crucial to success.

First, cut off and wire the stems before drying, as for strawflowers; afterward, the flowers shatter easily while handling. Use an airtight container with a lid, such as a Christmas

cookie tin. Spread about an inch of silica gel or other drying agent over the bottom, and place the flower heads face up on the surface; bend the wire stems at a sharp angle so that the flower will sit into the container. Then slowly pour the desiccant over and around the flower, covering all the petals and crevices and supporting it in its natural shape. Several flowers of the same kind can be dried in the same container as long as they do not touch one another. (Flowers of the same kind will dry more or less at the same time and can be removed in one operation.) Close, tape, label, and date the container and put it in a warm, dry place. Check it in two or three days. Remove blooms from the desiccant on just the right day; otherwise, they will be ruined.

Because flowers dried in silica gel will reabsorb moisture very rapidly in humid conditions, they must be stored in sealed, airtight containers, and displayed only in a dry atmosphere. (Floral craft shops carry silica gel; it is expensive, but it can be reactivated in the oven and used over and over.)

Sand is cheap and easy to obtain. Fine white sand, such as that used for children's sandboxes, is good; beach sand or sand from other natural sources should be washed, screened, and thoroughly dried. While flowers in silica gel will dry within a week or several days, drying in sand will take from about ten days to three weeks at room temperature. There is no need to worry

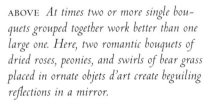

ABOVE *At times two or more single bouquets grouped together work better than one large one. Here, two romantic bouquets of dried roses, peonies, and swirls of bear grass placed in ornate objets d'art create beguiling reflections in a mirror.*

FACING PAGE *Evergreen branches enjoy a long tradition as indoor winter decorations. In this sprightly Christmas decoration for the foyer, evergreen and berried branches from the garden are actuated by tropical protea from the florist and Lady apples. The swag, made of white pine, box, cedar, and juniper snippings, adds vertical and horizontal dimension.*

about removing the flowers at exactly the right time, as with the gel method.

Any kind of container without a cover—a cardboard box, shoebox, or plastic container—will do for holding the sand. Follow the same basic procedure as that for silica gel. Place the open box of sand in a warm, dry place for about a week before checking the flowers. When the flowers are dry, either leave them in the sand, or if you need the container, store them in boxes the same way as for air-dried flowers.

Speedy drying can be achieved by placing the container of silica gel or sand in a warm oven; this technique also provides better color and texture. According to Georgia Vance in *The Decorative Art of Dried Flower Arrangement*, tulips, peonies, and dahlias, among others, will dry beautifully in silica gel at 100°F in about 48 hours. The results can be so striking that perfecting this technique in your own kitchen is worth the effort. And because the process is faster, you can dry many more flowers in the same amount of time than you could with ordinary drying methods.

Microwave-drying is the fastest method and, when successful, gives the best results. However, experimentation is required to discover the technique that will work best with your particular microwave model. A single half-opened rose dries beautifully when zapped at full power for one minute in my Litton Futura

BELOW *Dried flowers can be used in ways that are impractical for fresh flowers. The festive, long-lasting, and reusable wreath and topiaries shown here are created by attaching dried flowers and foliage to a base with a glue gun and bedecking them with ribbons and glittery ornaments. Roses, peonies, white delphinium, celosia, and flat eucalyptus can be harvested and dried from the garden, and fill-ins from the florist can provide the finishing touches.*

FACING PAGE *The brightly colored blooms in this dried arrangement on a nineteenth-century washstand at the Woodrow Wilson Birthplace and Museum in Staunton, Virginia, look fresh and natural. Although many flowers can be air-dried with good results, most of the larger, more delicate blooms such as these keep better form and color if they are dried in sand or silica gel.*

microwave oven. I set the bloom on top of silica gel in the bottom of a paper cup, completely cover it with more gel to the top, and place a cup of water toward the back of the oven. If you are venturesome, check your owner's manual first before trying your own experiments. You will, of course, have to forgo wiring stems ahead of time and wait until the silica gel has cooled before removing the flower.

DRYING FOLIAGE

Foliage is difficult to dry, but leaves treated with glycerin are long lasting and supple. Expect the color to change as the leaves absorb the glycerin; various shades of gold, beige, green, and mahogany will result. The effect is often heavy, but heavy is not necessarily bad and can make a dried display distinctive.

Use only mature leaves in good condition; pick them in midseason. Fill a jar about three-fourths full with a mixture of one part glycerin (available in drugstores and reusable) and three parts hot water. Crush woody stem ends and stand them in the jar. Check the level of the solution frequently, and replenish it as necessary to keep the crushed ends covered. When all parts of the leaves have turned color, they're done. Wipe off any beads of glycerin with a damp cloth and hang the foliage upside down for a few days to finish drying.

Leaves with a thin texture respond best to pressing. Ferns, hostas, and the swordlike foliage of irises and grasses give excellent results. Some-

times it's necessary to glue leaves back onto a stem if they fall off during pressing. The simplest way, that is, without a press made of boards, is to place leaves without overlapping them between sheets of newspaper or blotting paper. Several layers can be made, alternating foliage and paper. Put something heavy on top of the stack and leave it in a warm, dry place for several weeks. You can also press a few leaves in a telephone book or under the carpet in an out-

of-the-way area. The foliage will be crisp; take care in handling it.

Dried Flower Arranging

Many of the guidelines that apply to creating fresh flower arrangements also apply to making dried ones, with a few differences. Unlike fresh flowers, which continue to develop for a time in a container of water, thereby bringing interest and excitement to the arrangement, dried flowers are static. Boredom

A freestyle contemporary arrangement melds with a painted terra-cotta tripod vase to evoke an autumnal mood. The open design uses a restricted palette of tawny grass, brown dock from the fields, green seedpods of baptisia, and hydrangea.

suitable for dried arrangements, and there are other possibilities, since water leakage is not a problem. Baskets and wooden containers, earthenware and terra-cotta also have an affinity for dried flowers. A sculptured piece of wood or metal can be made into a container or base for a contemporary arrangement, and dried material can be wired to it.

Another alternative is to make a bouquet that is flat on one side and lay it on a woven tray as a centerpiece, or directly on the table. The bouquet may be made by bunching the flowers in your hand. Start with the largest and add the smaller kinds, one at a time, paying attention to overall color and shape. Take care to nestle the flowers one by one without breaking the rigid stems. Then tie the stems together with pipe cleaners or raffia and cut them to a single length. A round bouquet can be created in similar fashion and displayed either in a container or alone, supported by its own stems.

To make an arrangement in a container, begin by weighting the container with sand or stones. Insert chicken wire or floral foam—the type made specifically for dried flowers—as a base into which you will anchor the flower stems; secure the foam to the container with floral tape. A brown foam designed for dried flowers is strong enough to support large stems without crumbling. Ordinary Styrofoam will hold light or wire stems satisfactorily. The foam should protrude a few inches above the top of the container to

can be prevented by creating many mini-compositions to blend into the larger design so that there will always be something new to discover about it. The nice thing about working with preserved material is that you can take your own sweet time about finishing it, giving you the opportunity to make thoughtful adjustments of color, shape, and materials as you go along.

The same containers that are favorites for fresh flowers may also be

allow some flowers and foliage to cascade over the side.

As with fresh arrangements, insert stems by angling them toward an imaginary main focal point, starting with the heavier flowers, foliage, or branches. Fill in with smaller, fluffier material, turning your arrangement as you work and keeping in mind whether it will be seen on all sides. At the same time, try for a pleasing balance of complementary and contrasting shapes, colors, and textures. Wire smaller flowers together in bundles so that they will be easier to work with, and insert them as single elements in your composition. Save your main focal material—the dazzler peonies, dahlias, or roses—until last. When finished, spritz the arrangement with hair spray or a floral sealant to help preserve it and to set any petals that might have loosened.

Forcing Branches

In addition to making winter arrangements using dried flowers, you can sample a hint of spring as early as January or February by forcing branches from certain garden shrubs and trees to bloom indoors. "Forcing" is a harsh word for what is actually a gentle procedure. It involves cutting dormant branches from spring-flowering shrubs and fruit trees, bringing them indoors, and placing them in water. All you need are sharp pruners, a deep bucket of water in which to stand the cut

Black wheat and spikes of lavender create twin architectural table arrangements that mingle easily with other styles. The square black lacquered pots and the gold mesh ribbons are formal touches. The same dried material in round terra-cotta pots and gingham ribbons could lend country accents to another setting.

branches, and a cool, well-lit place out of direct sunlight in which to hold them while buds fatten, perhaps a garage or a sun porch.

Branches can be cut at almost any time after the winter solstice here in the Northeast, but cut them three to six weeks before you will want flowers and at least five weeks before the normal bloom time of the plant. The optimum time to cut branches is when the flower buds, which are larger than leaf buds, are just beginning to swell. This varies from plant to plant, and the weather plays a role as well. Through experience, you'll soon be able to decide the best time for cutting.

In general, it's best to start with the earliest bloomers—the various witch hazels, winter honeysuckle, pussy willows, star magnolia, forsythias, and flowering quinces— then flowering fruit trees and other shrubs. Try some species with inconspicuous flowers, catkins, or tender young foliage for out-of-the-ordinary displays—weeping willows, beeches, maples, hazelnuts, alders, cornelian cherry, and spicebush, for example.

Prune to maintain the shape of the shrub or tree as well as for the shapes of the branches you want to force. Make a clean cut flush with a major branch on a shrub, just outside the branch collar on a tree. When you bring the branches inside, scrape off a few inches of the bark above the lower end, and either make several vertical slits in it or crush it to aid water uptake. Then

submerge the branches in tepid water for several hours or rinse them to free them of dust and insects and put them directly in a deep container of room-temperature water in bright, but not direct, light. At this point, you can either arrange the branches and put them on view to watch them come into flower (a treat in itself) or keep them in a bucket in a humid place until the buds are plump. If you choose the latter course, keep the temperature on the cool side, 50–60° F. Covering the branches with a plastic dry-cleaner's bag and tying it around the top of the bucket will provide a moist greenhouse atmosphere that is perfect for developing buds. When the buds show color, arrange them and put them on display as the first welcome heralds of spring from your garden.

Forsythias deserve further mention. They are among the most popular shrubs in northern gardens and among the easiest to force. They are durable, feisty growers and are not fussy about soil. Their flower buds open before their leaves in early spring. They are easy to propagate, so easy that forced branches often root in the vase and can be planted out in the garden or in pots. Several cultivars of *Forsythia* × *intermedia* with choice flowers that make dramatic, sunny displays are 'Lynwood Gold', 'Spring Glory', and 'Beatrix Farrand'. Cultivars of *F. suspensa*, a pendant form from China, are commonly grown and also have showy flowers.

Forced branches of forsythia in an antique gilded pitcher bring a sunny burst of spring to a bathroom in early February. With little trouble for the pleasure they bring, branches of many early flowering shrubs and small trees can be cut and forced into bloom indoors weeks before their natural blooming time.

PLANT
PROFILES

Every list of the "best" cut flowers is personal and unique. Following is only a limited selection of my favorites, except for the free-flowering annuals that are so wonderful and essential for bouquets. They are included in the appendix along with other excellent plants that can be cut for arrangements. Zonal information given indicates the northern limit of a plant's hardiness range.

SPRING/EARLY SUMMER

ALLIUM. *Ornamental onion.* A. afla-tunense, to 3½', Z4; A. caeruleum (*blue globe*), to 1½', Z4. A. christophii (*stars of Persia*), to 2', Z4; A. giganteum (*giant onion*), to 4', Z4. *Full sun to light shade. Average soil.*

Alliums produce small, medium, and large globular flower heads of tiny florets, offering nice round forms for cutting and lasting about ten days. They are notorious self-seeders and it's a good idea to remove uncut seed heads before they ripen.

The royal purple spheres of *Allium aflatunense* 'Purple Sensation',

four inches across, are a good all-around size. They appear in May, a little earlier than the globes of the similar, slightly taller *A. giganteum*. Both have strong stems and are desirable cut flowers. *A. caeruleum* has clear blue globes, two inches across; it's a lovely thing, especially when used with gray, chartreuse, or cream-variegated foliage. *A. christophii*, the best ornamental onion for the garden, blooms later than those mentioned, putting up enormous spheres, about a foot in diameter, of lilac, starry blooms on stout stems. The seed heads—spiky balls with three shiny black seeds in each "star-let"—are perfect for winter displays; save one to put on top of the Christmas tree.

Cut alliums when about half the florets on a flower head have opened and condition in cold water overnight. The oniony scent given off by alliums when they are bruised or crushed offends some people. The smell usually dissipates during conditioning and can be neutralized further by changing the vase water frequently; also rubbing with baking soda will take it off your hands.

Alliums with compact flower and seed heads dry well. Stand them in an inch or two of water in a warm place until dry, then finish them off by hanging them upside down for a few days. Hang seed heads upside down to dry without touching. Seed heads also dry nicely *in situ* during a dry spell in the garden, but mind their tendency to self-sow.

AQUILEGIA. *Columbine.* A. canadensis (*wild columbine*), to 2', Z3; A. × hybrida, to 3', Z5. *Full sun, but protect them from noonday sun where summers are brutal. Ordinary well-drained soil. NOTE: Seeds and all parts of the plant are poisonous.*

Aquilegias bloom after the spring bulb show, dancing on curiously spurred flowers on wiry stems above lacey green leaves. Sprays of dainty crimson-and-yellow flowers of *Aquilegia canadensis*, gathered from the wilder parts of the garden where they self-sow, are beguiling, but the larger-flowered hybrids, some four inches across, are better choices for cutting and showier in borders. 'McKana Giants' hybrids, with long-spurred flowers and strong stems are

among the best for cutting; they come in a dazzling array of bicolors—blue, white, pink, red, violet, and yellow. They bloom for a month or more, but tend to be short-lived, so put in a few new plants each year. I also like the spurless 'Nora Barlow' as a novelty, although it is an old form with double flowers in shades of red, pink, and a lovely soft green. It is notably strong-stemmed, and provides brilliant red autumnal foliage good for picking. Some nurseries carry plants; otherwise seeds are available from Monticello in Virginia. (See Sources.)

Cut columbines when half the flowers on a stem are open; buds that show color will continue to open in water. Condition in cool water overnight. For drying, treat in silica gel for three or four days.

BULBS. Chionodoxa *(glory-of-the-snow)*, Z4; Muscari *(grape hyacinth)*, Z2; Scilla *(squill)*, Z4; Hyacinthoides hispanica *(Spanish bluebells)*, Z4; Hy-

acinthus orientalis *(hyacinth)*, Z4; Fritillaria meleagris *(checkered fritillary)*, Z4. *Sun, or light shade under trees and shrubs. Rich soil for best results, except for* Fritillaria meleagris, *which likes gritty, well-drained soil.*

Glory-of-the-snow (*Chionodoxa* spp.), grape hyacinth (*Muscari* spp.), and squills (*Scilla* spp.) are among the so-called "minor bulbs" with short but cuttable stems; they are long lasting in winter and lift one's spirits at the end of the winter season. Their dominant color is blue, but white and pink forms are available as well. Arrange these by handfuls, or use them to create a spring "garden" in a basket or shallow dish.

Spanish bluebells (*Hyacinthoides hispanica*), related to squills, are a little taller with flower stalks between 10 and 15 inches high, making them excellent cut flowers. They come in single colors of blue ('Blue Queen'), white ('White Triumphator'), and pink ('Dainty Maid').

The large heads of hyacinths (*Hyacinthus orientalis*) in a vase by themselves are quite superb, and their heavy perfume will fill a room. Hyacinth 'Delft Blue', 'Carnegie' (white), and 'Anne Marie' (pink) are lovely, and also good for forcing. 'Jan Bos' is close to a true red.

My favorite fritillary is the appealing checkered *F. meleagris*, with nodding, solitary blooms in purple, gray, bronze, or white on foot-high stems that are slender but strong. Arrange them simply, to show off each individual flower.

Cut flowers as soon as they are safely beyond the tight bud stage. If flowers of short-stemmed varieties are mud-spattered, gently swish them around in a pan of tepid water while holding the stems. Cut on a diagonal with a sharp knife. Remove or slit any white pulp at the base of stems, and condition stems in cold water. Most will remain in good shape from several days to more than a week. For the greatest longevity, change water frequently and recut the taller stems.

DIANTHUS. *Pinks.* D. barbatus *(sweet William, biennial), to 2', Z3;* D. deltoides, *to 1½', Z3. Sun;* D. deltoides *is shade-tolerant. Fast-draining neutral or alkaline soil.*

In June, foot-high clumps of the old maiden pink (*Dianthus deltoides*) send out their mauve, white, and red toothed or "pinked" blossoms. About an inch across, they grow on forked stems above slender grassy

foliage. They are not as spicy as the cottage pinks (*D. plumarius*) and all-woodii hybrids that sport their variously fringed and patterned petals in borders later in summer, but they create sweet bouquets when mixed with frothy sprays of lady's-mantle and columbines (*Aquilegia canadensis*).

The best pink for cutting, however, is sweet William (*D. barbatus*), usually grown as a biennial, which blooms for several weeks in the garden and is also long lasting as a cut flower. It is less fragrant but taller than most other pinks, with stout stems and showy flat-topped flower clusters. Varicolored cultivars such as 'Indian Carpet' provide rich mosaic patterns for dazzling bouquets, but I rely on the old standby 'Newport Pink', which always pleases, whether its rich salmon-pink flowers are arranged by themselves, with its white sibling 'White Beauty', or in mixed displays.

Cut stems of short-stemmed pinks when one or two flowers in a cluster have opened and buds are fat; they will continue to open. Handfuls can be placed immediately in water in pewter mugs, china cups, or small vases as finished bouquets. Cut flowers of sweet William when half the florets in a cluster are open; recut stems on a slant and make a single vertical slit in the sturdier ones; condition overnight in tepid water. Flowers last ten days or longer. Press individual blooms for flower pictures.

DICENTRA. *Bleeding-heart.* D. eximia (*wild or fringed bleeding-heart*), to 2';

D. formosa (*western bleeding-heart*), to 2'; D. spectabilis, to 3'. All Z3. Part or bright shade; tolerates sun in mild climates. Rich, moist, humusy soil.

Bleeding-hearts are endearing old-fashioned perennials, with dangling sprays of rosy pink, or white heart-shaped flowers on arching stems. They bloom well ahead of most perennials. The classic *Dicentra spectabilis* is the best for cutting, and 'Alba', the white form, is the aristocrat of bleeding-hearts. Sadly, *D. spectabilis* blooms for a relatively short time, and may close up shop altogether by midsummer, to reappear again the following spring. But this is an insufficient reason to banish it from your garden. (Surround it with hostas or late perennials as camouflage.)

Fringed and western bleeding-heart (*D. eximia* and *D. formosa*, respectively) are more tolerant of direct sun, will bloom sporadically over the summer, and if given ample moisture, the finely dissected grayish or bluish foliage will stay neat where summers are not long and hot.

Cut sprays when about half the flowers on a stem are open. The lovely foliage of fringed and western bleeding-heart can be cut sparingly to use with its flowers, but do not cut leaves from *D. spectabilis*, as this will weaken it. To condition, dip the fleshy stems in a few inches of hot water for several seconds, then fill the container with cold water, allowing the flowers to stand for a few hours before arranging. Or simply

condition overnight in cool water. Flowers will last several days.

The flower stems do not dry successfully, but small sprays can be dried for pressed-flower pictures.

DIGITALIS. *Foxglove.* D. grandiflora, to 2', Z3; D. lutea, to 3', Z3; D. purpurea (*biennial*), to 5', Z4; Sun or light shade. Rich, moist, humusy soil. NOTE: Some species are poisonous.

Vertical lines are valuable in the garden and for indoor flower displays, and foxgloves help fill the bill at this time of year. I rely on two early-blooming perennial species for medium-sized bouquets where the spiky form and tubular flowers of foxgloves are wanted on a more delicate scale than that of the common foxglove. *Digitalis grandiflora* is a short clump-former, with pale yellow flowers veined in brown. The other, *D. lutea*, bears slender stems of small greeny yellow flowers. Both look congenial in almost any setting.

The stately biennial, *D. purpurea*, commonly found in gardens, is better suited for larger-scale arrangements. Cultivars come in mixed shades of white, pink, mauve, and red, often leaning toward magenta, and have pretty speckles or blotches at their throats. I grow only the creamy white cultivar 'Alba', which has spotless tubelike flowers that look fresh and pure against any background. 'Alba' blooms a little later than the other cultivars, but like them, self-sows if allowed to go to seed in the garden.

Cut when half the flowers on the spike are open. They will keep longer if placed in warm water, to 100°F, and left to cool in the same water overnight. (If stalks are too long, break them off at the length you want.) To dry, place stalks lengthwise in silica gel. Air-dry seed heads.

HELLEBORUS. *Hellebore. H. foetidus (stinking hellebore), to 1½'; H. niger (Christmas rose), to 1'; H. orientalis (Lenten rose), to 1½'. All Z3. Consistent light shade is best, or under deciduous shrubs or trees. Damp, rich, nearly neutral soil. NOTE: Poisonous plants.*

Hellebores will bloom in winter or early spring when little else in the garden does. The porcelain white blooms, four inches across, of the Christmas rose (*Helleborus niger*) can be found nodding on short stems in my Zone 6 garden sometime in March, when they can be snipped to float in a bowl, or made into a small arrangement. The Lenten hellebore

(*H. orientalis*) appears a week or two later, with dusty rose and maroon flowers. Hybrids are showier than the species, ranging in color from cream through pink and darkest plum purple, often with a greenish tinge and beautiful markings. Some say it is the best of all hellebores and the easiest to grow.

My favorite is *H. foetidus*, which despite its wretched name, is uncommonly beautiful with apple green clusters of flowers edged in burgundy. It will sometimes bloom in February, if there is a thaw. It has green-black fingered leaves, the handsomest of any hellebore. To maintain a healthy colony the evergreen leaves of hellebores should not be picked at this time of year, or picked only sparingly if the temptation is irresistible.

Cut hellebores when the flowers become papery. Split the stems of Christmas rose and *H. foetidus* and condition overnight in cold water. The Lenten rose can be tempera-

mental if not properly conditioned. Either make a shallow slit along the length of the stem, or prick the stems with a pin in several places. Then stand stems in cold water up to their heads. Keep the arrangement away from heat. Use a desiccant to dry flowers. Dry seed heads by standing stems in a few inches of water.

IRIS. *Iris. Bearded iris, to 4½', Z3; I. sibirica (Siberian iris) to 3½', Z3; Most prefer sun, some take partial shade. Bearded irises require well-drained soil; Siberian irises need moisture retentive, but not wet, soil.*

Bearded and Siberian irises have strong-stemmed showy flowers and attractive blade-like foliage and are among the finest irises for cutting. Bearded irises are available in different heights and bloom times, with flowers in a fantastic range of colors. The petals and beard can be all the same color, or a blend of similar tones, or in contrasting colors. Many exciting combinations are offered, but for arranging, irises in uniform colors and tender shades of blue, lavender, and soft yellows are always good. In selecting irises, try to see them blooming to assure you get the colors you want.

Beardless Siberian irises have shapely flowers from two to six inches across with velvety petals and slender grassy foliage. Select a white and a blue variety and you will have an abundance of blooms for cutting. I grow 'Snow Queen', and the lovely 'Flight of Butterflies' with fretted

veins of light blue on dark blue petals. 'Butter and Yellow' has bright yellow falls and white standards.

Cut when the first bud is nearly open; buds lower down on the stem will open somewhat smaller. Condition in room temperature water for several hours or overnight. Irises are sensitive to sudden temperature changes and should not be brought from the garden into a cold room. Individual blooms last only a day or two; pick off each blossom as it fades to keep the bouquet looking fresh and to encourage other buds to open. The foliage can be used in bouquets all summer. The flowers of bearded irises are too perishable to dry. Seedpods of many irises are wonderful for dried bouquets.

PAEONIA. *Peony.* P. lactiflora *(common garden peony, Chinese peony), to 3½', Z2. Sun. Deep, enriched soil.*

All peonies are gorgeous and make superb cut flowers. Single varieties in general have stronger stems than doubles, but their flowers do not last quite as long in the garden or the vase. The doubles have crinkled or ruffled flounces of petals in huge bowls of bloom. The Japanese types and other singles have satiny saucerlike blooms with fewer rows of petals, and are decorated at the center with great bosses of golden stamens, or ribbonlike petals which are greatly admired in bouquets where they are seen up close.

'Festiva Maxima' is the best double white, with strong stems, a heady fragrance and glistening petals flecked with crimson. I also like 'Sarah Bernhardt', which is cotton-candy pink, and ruby red 'Felix Crouse'. These antique peonies provide a succession of gorgeous blooms for cutting from early June to July. 'Honey Gold' is another superior choice for cutting.

Among the singles I would choose 'Krinkled White', 'Gold Standard', and 'Seashell', an iridescent pink. Good semidoubles are 'Pink Lemonade' with cream, yellow, and pink blended into each bloom, and 'Coral Charm', a rich apricot.

Cut stems when the buds are about half open and showing color; leave at least two strong sets of leaves remaining on each stalk to strengthen the plant for next year's bloom. For the same reason, do not pick more than half the buds from a plant in a season. Slit the stems an inch or two vertically, and put them in cold water overnight or until the blossoms are as open as you like. For a future special occasion, the blooms can be held in limbo for a few weeks in a plastic bag in the refrigerator, at about 50°F, then taken out and arranged.

The flowers are a challenge to dry. Use either silica gel combined with oven heat, or the silica gel/microwave technique, if you can find the right equation; begin with low power at one to three minutes. The foliage takes up glycerin well and will turn a burgundy bronze.

PAPAVER. *Poppy.* P. orientale *(Oriental poppy), to 4', Z3. Sun. Deeply dug, moist but light soil.*

Oriental poppies are showoffs, but used with restraint and properly conditioned they are gorgeous cut flowers that last several days. Their flamboyant, crepe-petaled flower goblets (up to ten inches across), fashioned with dark blotches and bosses of stamens and wheellike seed capsules are no longer confined to brilliant vermilion, which remains the most exciting color nonetheless, effective when used by itself. Modern cultivars include shades of orange, scarlet, red, pink, melon, gold, and white, and grow from two-and-a-half to three feet. Aside from 'Oriental' and 'Bonfire' in the hot-red category, I like lovely 'Helen Elizabeth', soft pink, unblotched, and easy to arrange with other flowers, and 'Barr's White', an elegant white poppy with black splotches at the base of the petals. 'Victoria Dreyfus' is also appealing with salmon blooms edged in silver and strong wiry stems.

Poppies in general have stout stems with a tendency to sprawl and should be staked. Also their leaves turn yellow and disappear by August; some type of camouflage should be provided to cover the gap, perhaps planting them in front of baby's-breath or asters, which will lean over the bare spots.

Cut stems when the buds are fat and beginning to unfold. Recut stems to the desired length and immediately plunge them into a few inches of boiling water for about ten seconds, or char several inches of the stem ends over a very hot flame (preferably gas); this prevents the milky sap from clogging the water-conducting cells in the stems and causing the flowers to droop prematurely. Then stand them in deep cold water for several hours or overnight. If stems are recut during arranging, they must be seared again.

SYRINGA. *Lilac.* Shrub. S. × persica *(Persian lilac) to 8', Z3;* S. vulgaris *(common lilac) and hybrids, to 20', Z3. Sun. Well-drained limy soil.*

To awaken in spring with the scent of cut lilac branches wafting through the house is one of life's sweet pleasures. Some modern cultivars have little or no fragrance, but in addition to the classic lilac color, they offer flower colors in white, pink, red, blue, and deep purple. A few among the many cultivars of *Syringa vulgaris* that have stood the test of time are 'Vestale', a single white, and 'Ellen Willmott', a double white. 'President Lincoln' is the best of the blue lilacs; 'Sensation' has single purplish burgundy florets edged in white; and 'Charm' is a single pink. 'Lavender Lady' is reliable in northern and southern gardens. Properly grown, the smaller-proportioned Persian lilacs, all under ten feet, virtually cover themselves with a mass of fragrant lilac flowers in small panicles measuring about three inches long and wide—a fine shrub for smaller gardens and lovely when cut and arranged.

Cut branches when one-third to one-half of the flower panicle is open. Strip off the leaves, split or hammer the stems at the base, then place stem ends in hot water, and allow to stand overnight. For foliage, cut a few nonflowering branches to mix with the flowers in bouquets, and replace them as they droop. Glorious bouquets result from mixing blue, purple, or white lilacs with delphiniums and lupines, while white is a classic for weddings. Dry lilacs in sand or borax for minimum fading and shrinking. In silica gel, two or three days should be ample; avoid overdrying. Many kinds will keep their fragrance for a time after drying.

SUMMER

ACHILLEA. *Yarrow.* A. *'Coronation Gold', to 3'; A. filipendulina (fern-leaf yarrow) to 5'; A. millefolium, to 1½'; A. 'Moonshine', to 2'. All Z3. Sun. Ordinary garden soil on the dry, lean side.*

The yarrows mentioned here are a joy to grow and among the best flowers for both fresh and dried bouquets. They have large, platelike flower heads, up to five inches across, which will provide months of flowers if they are kept cut. They bloom bountifully in sun, are drought-resistant, and low maintenance.

'Coronation Gold' and 'Moonshine' are two of the most familiar cultivars. The first bears chrome yellow three-inch flower plates on long strong stems. 'Moonshine', a little shorter, puts out sulfur yellow corymbs above finely-cut, silvery gray foliage, and is the prettiest of the yellow yarrows. *Achillea filipen-*

dulina 'Gold Plate' has six-inch flower heads and makes a fine tall companion with ornamental grasses.

Many hybrids developed from *A. millefolium* are available in new hues ranging from yellow, salmon, lavender, and ruby red to creamy white. They are easily grown from seed, and will flower the first year if seeds are sown indoors in early spring. They are useful to fill gaps in the garden, effective planted in masses, and provide winsome flat round flower heads in a variety of colors for country bouquets.

Cut yarrow when about half the buds on the flower head are open. Condition overnight; the blooms will last a week to ten days. To dry, hang the stalks upside down, or let them stand in a jug with several inches of water until dry. Take care that their heads do not touch. They dry quickly and will keep good color and shape, but cultivars of *A. mille-folium* do not dry as well as the other yarrows mentioned.

ALCHEMILLA. *Lady's-mantle.* A. *mollis, to 2', Z3; A. vulgaris, to 1½', Z 3. Sun or partial shade. Appreciates moist soil. NOTE: There is confusion surrounding its name, with nurseries offering the same plant as both* Alchemilla mollis *and* A. vulgaris.

Lady's-mantle, with its charming way of creeping along and raising its frothy chartreuse plumes among neighboring plants, is a must for gardens and bouquets. Its lobed and pleated leaves, which cup morning dew and raindrops in the garden, are equally winning when mixed into bouquets. Catalogs are offering an "improved form" with neater, more upright, and larger flowers.

The delicate flower sprays rise above the leaves in June and last through August, and when cut will hold up in water for about two weeks. Their intense greenish yellow green color acts as a foil for sedate blue, white, peach pinks, and pale yellows; those with an artist's eye mix it in garden and bouquets with reds (especially red roses) and oranges. The leaves can be picked all season, but they are not as long-lived in water as the flowers. If the leaves look worn out by midsummer or become host to spider mites—both often resulting from a lack of ample moisture—simply cut them off and a fresh crop will appear in a few weeks.

No special conditioning is required, but I leave flowers to drink for a few hours before arranging in room temperature water. The small blossoms air-dry nicely; either hang them or arrange them in a vase with water and enjoy them as they dry.

ASTILBE. *Astilbe, garden spirea.* A. japonica, *to 3′, Z4;* A. thunbergii, *to 3′, Z4;* A. × hybrida *and cultivars, to over 3′, Z4. Most will thrive in part shade, or sun, in rich, moist soil.*

Any of the many *Astilbe × hybrida* provide fine tapering panicles for cutting, and they can be selected to give you flowers from June to September. The spiky blooms, about a foot long and covered with countless tiny flowers, require no staking. They bloom in feathery pyramids, weeping plumes, and stiff upright forms. The foliage of shiny divided leaves comes in a range of tints from bright green to bronze—a handsome addition to arrangements with or without the flowers.

Make selections according to desired color and bloom time, early, midseason, or late. Those that bloom in July and August are *A. japonica* 'Red Sentinel', with bright carmine flowers and reddish foliage, one of the few that will adapt to dry conditions; *A. j.* 'Rheinland', which has the best clear pink flowers for early July blooms; and *A. thunbergii* 'Ostrich Plume', which carries weep-

ing salmon pink plumes into August. *A. × hybrida* 'Snowdrift' has clearer white flowers than ivory *A. × h.* 'Avalanche', which I grow, but not its soft, loose form, which I prefer in arrangements.

Cut when half the flowers on a panicle are open. Pick foliage, too, which is attractive and long lasting. Split stems before standing in tepid water for several hours. They will keep a week or longer.

Pick for drying when almost all the florets on a panicle are open, and hang upside down. Flowers shrink considerably during drying, but retain good form and color. Shrinkage is less with silica gel, or use borax or cornmeal. Both flowers and foliage press well. Rich brown seed plumes are decorative; pick before they shatter, hang upside down to finish drying; spray with a sealer.

BUDDLEIA. *Buddleia, butterfly bush.* Shrub. B. davidii, *to 20′, Z6; Sun. Fertile, well-drained neutral soil.*

These fast-growing shrubs give structure and jewel-tone flowers of white, lavender, and purple to the summer garden, often continuing until frost. Butterflies are often seen hovering over them, drinking from the nectaries of the tiny florets that make up the flower spikes. The foliage, gray-green or blue-green stays handsome all season in the garden, but does not last well in water. In my Zone 6 garden the tops often die back in harsh winters, but emerge fat and sassy from their roots in spring, providing a dependable back-up supply of flowers for cutting.

Buddleia davidii cultivars and hybrids are the ones most commonly grown, and many selections are offered. There are several good white forms. I favor 'White Profusion' for its gracefully proportioned flower spikes from six to eight inches, which are not overpowering in arrangements. 'Empire Blue' is the closest to a true blue, and reputed to be exceptionally long lasting when cut. 'Black Knight' has striking blue-black flowers for creative arrangements (try mixing them with white 'Casa Blanca' lilies), and 'Royal Red', actually magenta, is the best "red" buddleia. 'Nanho Blue' and 'Nanho Purple' are compact shrubs that are good choices for small borders or gardens.

Although some say that buddleia makes an excellent cut flower when properly conditioned, I find it erratic, usually lasting only a few days. The following method has given me the best results: Cut spikes when half open, but before bottom florets begin to fade. Strip off all foliage, dunk the stem ends into one inch of boiling water for a minute, and leave them in deep water for as long as possible. To dry, cut when spikes show good fresh color and place them lengthwise in silica gel or borax.

CAMPANULA. *Campanula, bellflower. C. lactiflora, to 4', Z5; C. latifolia, to 4', Z3; C. persicifolia (peach-leaved bellflower), to 3', Z3. Sun or part shade. Moist but well-drained neutral or slightly alkaline soil.*

Campanulas, from rock garden rosettes to the bold six-footers, are sterling undemanding plants with showy blue or white bell flowers, either solitary on the stems or in clusters. Several are excellent for cutting, with the peach-leaved bellflower unarguably the best. It blooms in June and July, producing one-and-a-half-inch cup-shaped blooms on slender upright stems, and lasts

about ten days in a vase. Cultivars abound, but my two favorites for cutting are 'Alba'; and 'Telham Beauty', which is a lovely soft blue. 'Blue Gardenia' and 'White Pearl' are doubles.

Campanula lactiflora, flowering from late spring to late summer, is also good for cutting and gives a different effect, carrying cone-shaped panicles of flowers at the tips of four-foot stalks. I favor 'Loddon Anna', in pale pink. *C. latifolia* 'Macrantha' also deserves mentioning, although it makes a capricious cut flower if not conditioned properly. It is a bold upright plant with electric purple-blue flowers on sturdy stalks, perfect for more formal arrangements.

Cut when several flowers on a stem are open; flower buds will continue to open in water. Condition peach-leaved bellflower in cool water for several hours. It will last a week or more. *C. lactiflora* and *C. latifolia* must have their stem ends seared over a flame or dipped in boiling water for about ten seconds, then conditioned overnight in warm water to start.

COREOPSIS. *Tickseed. C. grandiflora, to 2½', Z5; C. verticillata (thread-leaf coreopsis), to 3', Z3. Sun, but will tolerate some shade. Light sandy or loamy soil.*

Yellow-flowered daisies are a staple of many bouquets, and the cutting garden or border can hold a few clumps blooming at different times. Use *Coreopsis grandiflora* 'Sunray' as the

basis for yellow-and-white bouquets of nicotiana, white lilies, and assorted shades of yellow daisies. Its glowing yellow double flowers bloom from late June through August; it has healthy green leaves and strong stems that need no staking. If it is coddled with nutrients, rich soil, and moisture, however, it will sprawl and produce fewer flowers. Cut frequently to encourage flowering. The semidouble *C. g.* 'Early Sunrise' is also a good choice and will flower in its first year from seeds sown in early spring.

Thread-leaf coreopsis (*C. verticillata*) 'Moonbeam' is on everybody's ten-best list for the garden, and useful for cutting. With its finely dissected foliage and dainty yellow flowers on slender stems it plays a supporting role, acting as an elegant filler among more substantial blooms in both garden and bouquet. If, however, you love it enough to give it stage center, mass it by itself in a blue glass vase.

As with all daisies, cut flowers when they are newly open, but with centers still tight. Condition in deep water overnight. Flowers will last a week to ten days. Double flowers will dry well in silica gel. Individual blossoms of 'Moonbeam' can be pressed for flower pictures.

DELPHINIUM. *Delphinium. D. × belladonna, to 5', Z3; D. elatum hybrids, to 8', Z3; D. grandiflorum, to 2', Z3. Sun. Rich, neutral, well-drained soil.*

Stately true-blue and white delphiniums grow in everybody's dream garden. The tall *Delphinium elatum* Blackmore and Langdon strain and Pacific Coast hybrids are magnificent perennials in the garden, but they are demanding plants to grow well. Also, while their tall spikes of huge flowers are spectacular, they are not as practical for everyday arranging needs as the belladonna hybrids. These attractive shorter plants range from 30 inches to five feet and have

a loose informal shape and smaller (one-and-a-half to two-inch) florets that keep coming on all summer if flowers are kept cut. 'Connecticut Yankee' is the shortest, at 30 inches, bushy and free-flowering, with charming single flowers in white and a range of blues. 'Bellamosa' is almost navy blue, to four feet; and, 'Belladonna' is a light blue five-footer—the only one that might require some support.

Another good delphinium for cutting is *D. grandiflorum,* sometimes called Chinese delphinium. *D. g.* 'Blue Mirror' is short enough for the front of the border, has racemes of loose flowers in brilliant gentian-blue, and finely cut leaves which can be picked with the flowers. It, too, blooms all summer; however, it is a short-lived perennial, which should be treated as a biennial, or, as an annual by sowing seeds in early spring.

Pick blooms just before all the flowers are open along the stem, leaving a few buds at the top. Condition overnight in room-temperature water in a cool place; handle carefully as the flowers bruise easily. They will last for several days, and look great with phlox 'Miss Lingard' or soft yellow lilies. To dry, pick when about two-thirds of the flowers along the stems are open. Dry in silica gel, sand, or hang upside down to air-dry.

ECHINACEA. *Purple coneflower. E. purpurea, to 5', Z3; Sun. Prefers rich, moist, slightly acidic soil, but withstands dry conditions.*

A large-flowered daisy, purple coneflower is the purplish pink or white counterpart of yellow black-eyed Susan (*Rudbeckia* sp.). It is somewhat coarse but attractive, free-flowering and carefree—a boon to the busy gardener. Its distinctive, bold flowers have reflexed petals around a central brownish dome studded with stiff orange bracts. Flowering begins in late June and continues until frost. If the flowers are not cut, they seem to last forever, though the color fades. Butterflies (as well as deer, woodchucks, and rabbits) dote on them. They are eye-catching planted in groups in the border, provide a nonstop flower supply for cutting, and are good candidates for sunny meadows. They make excellent cut flowers, and the dried conical seed heads are fine ornaments for arranging.

My first choice is 'Bright Star', for its rosy pink rays and handsome maroon disks. Group it with either 'White Swan', which is clear white and slightly shorter, or with the warmer white, 'White Lustre', with bronze disks, planting two pink plants for every white for the best effect.

Cut it as for any daisy—when the flowers are fully open, but while the centers are still tight. Strip off leaves and condition for several hours. Use purple coneflower alone in bouquets with added greenery or in bold arrangements, perhaps with lilies and spiky white blazing star (*Liatris* sp.) or cimicifuga (*Cimicifuga* sp.). To dry, cut flower heads after the petals have dropped and seeds have formed; hang upside down to dry. Seed heads will dry naturally on the plant in dry weather.

LEUCANTHEMUM × superbum.
Shasta daisy, to 3', Z5. Mostly sun. Rich, well-drained soil.

Shastas, the quintessential daisy with large heads of showy white rays around a central eye, are extremely

useful whether featured by themselves in large bunches in bouquets, or mixed with other flowers. Flowers may be six inches across, as in 'Starburst' or 'Majestic'. Some are earlier to bloom than others, and many will continue blooming until frost if they are cut regularly.

There are many cultivars in singles, doubles, and shaggy flower heads. I choose singles or semidoubles for their clear shapes and versatility in bouquets. 'Alaska' bears perfectly formed three-to-four-inch single daisies on three-foot stems; shear it back after the first blooming and it will come back for an encore. 'Esther Read' is a well-known double, and 'Marconi' is superb if you fancy the double, frilled kinds. If you find pure white a little too stark, 'Cobham Gold' has ivory-colored double petals with a central cone of soft yellow.

Plants flourish with little care, save perhaps staking and dividing every couple of years to keep them vigorous. You can pinch back the stems to avoid staking, but the tradeoff is smaller flowers.

Cut when petals open, but while the central disk is fresh and tight. Condition overnight beginning with warm water. Split older stems that are woody. Because of their simple charm, daisies go well with earthenware jugs and other country containers, but are equally refreshing in a silver bowl. Single daisies are difficult to dry. If you are determined, pick when centers are open and glue petals before drying. Or experiment.

LILIUM.
Lily. Asiatic hybrids, to 5', Z3; Oriental hybrids, to 7', Z5; L. regale 'Album,' to 5', Z3; Trumpet and Aurelian hybrids, to 7', Z5. Sun or part shade. Any good garden soil with free drainage.

These are glamorous flowering bulbs with long, strong stems and long lasting flowers in a variety of forms and mouthwatering colors—actually every color except blue. A mature bulb of the taller varieties may produce as many as 50 flowers. Flowers of those mentioned here measure from about four inches across to about ten on the Oriental hybrids. Many are fragrant. They like a cool root run, and tall ones should be staked.

Among the many Asiatic hybrids, which bloom in June and July, 'Enchantment' is my first choice for its orangy red flowers with black speckles and an upward facing shape that is easy to arrange. A tidy three-foot plant carries about 16 medium-sized blooms, and a single cut stem often serves as a self-made bouquet. I also like 'Harlequin Hybrids', in mixed colors, with their whimsical swept-back petals and smallish pendant flowers. The sweetly scented regal lily (*Lilium regale* 'Album') furnishes a splendid supply of satiny white flowers with a golden central blush for more formal bouquets.

A classic among the trumpet lilies and the next to bloom, is 'Black Dragon'; it grows to seven feet, and produces sculpted funnel-shaped flowers, white and yellow inside, purply-brown on the reverse. Also at

this time, 'Lady Anne', a lovely Aurelian five-footer, offers flaring blooms in soft apricot blending to ivory. The exotic, spicy scented oriental lilies bloom throughout August. They are all impressive, but I lean toward those of the large flowered Imperial strain; spotted and banded petals in white, deep pink, crimson, and yellow edged in white have a good open-face form for bouquets. Grow at least one 'Casa Blanca' lily for sensational ten-inch bowls of unspotted white flowers with flashy orange anthers.

When cutting lilies leave at least one-half of the leafy stem behind if you want strong plants in years to come; or plant twice as many and cut only every other year from the same plant. Select stems when at least two of the lower buds are opening; the others will open successively in water over a long period. Take care not to bruise the petals. Split the stems and recut under water, then condition in warm water. They

will last as long as eight days when arranged. To prevent the falling pollen from ripened anthers from marring petals, furniture, and clothing, snip them off if you have the heart; or place the arrangement on a wipeable surface, such as glass or formica. Brush the pollen from fabric or wood with a *dry* sponge or cloth.

Lilies with thick or short broad petals dry better than recurved ones. Cover freshly opened buds in silica gel; let stand four to five days, or up to two days in silica gel in a slow oven.

MONARDA. *Monarda, wild bergamot. M. didyma (bee balm), to 3', Z4. Sun or light shade. Best in rich, moist soil.*

Monardas feature shaggy bright blossoms, about two inches across, at the ends of leafy stalks. The flowers make delightful cut flowers and the lush aromatic foliage is highly useful, lasting over a week when cut and placed in water; the flowers will

last about five days. Monardas belong to the mint family, and like their cousins, they are invasive. On balance, they make a lovely statement in the border, where they can be restrained, and in wild gardens, where they can be given their head.

The cultivar 'Cambridge Scarlet' provides brilliant intense red in the garden, the color that attracts hummingbirds. 'Adam' is a dark rich red, 'Blue Stocking' is violet-purple, and the colors of 'Croftway Pink', 'Mahogany', 'Snow Queen', and 'Violet Queen' are self-evident.

Monardas are susceptible to mildew, but the pink hybrid 'Marshall's Delight' has been bred to overcome this problem. Also dividing plants every spring will give healthier plants and assure lavish blooms.

Cut monardas when blooms begin to open. Condition overnight starting in warm water. A pleasing contrast results by arranging blossoms with purple-leaved foliage of smokebush (*Cotinus coggygria*) or barberry. Monardas also make lovely bouquets when mixed with the textured foliage and flower stalks of many herbs. Hang stalks upside-down to dry; the red cultivars will lose much of their vibrancy. Seed heads are good, too.

ROSA. *Rose.* Shrub. *David Austin's "English" Roses. Sun. Moisture retentive humusy soil.*

Although my preference in roses runs toward the old shrub roses, which I use lavishly in bouquets despite their short cut-flower life, the antique-rose look, fragrance, and expanded color range of the "English" roses, developed by the English breeder, David Austin, are earning permanent places in my garden and arrangements. They have been bred to be disease and pest resistant, but this is still on trial; unlike most shrub roses, which put out one flush of blooms in June, they provide roses all summer. The most exciting cultivar is Graham Thomas, named for the noted British plantsman, combining a rich gold color with a distinctive cup shape that is impossible not to cut, despite the prevailing wisdom that shrubs should not be pruned for two years after planting while they build up growth. Also impressive is Othello, a dark crimson velvety rose with a yellow center, the sturdiest (and thorniest) stemmed of all with handsome dusky foliage. Mary Rose is many-petalled with

deep pink blooms, quartered in the way of old roses. Each has an elusive fragrance, will repeat blooming throughout the summer, and grows to five feet and over. Each lasts several days in water; with floral preservative up to a week.

Cut stems of these shrub roses flush with a branch. (Cut stems of hybrid tea roses about one-quarter of an inch above a five-leaflet outward-facing leaf.) Choose roses at advanced bud stage, or, for more interest, at different stages of development. Remove unnecessary foliage and lower thorns. Split the ends vertically, or recut the stems on a slant; allow them to stand overnight in warm water up to their necks. (Or recut stems and dip them in boiling water for a minute, then stand in cold water for several hours.) If roses wilt prematurely, recut the stems under water and submerge heads and all for an hour or so. Arrange roses in masses with different shades of one color, or as focal points in mixed bouquets.

Preserve rosebuds and blooms in silica gel, or dry individual blooms in silica gel in the microwave. Collect and dry fragrant rose petals for potpourri on trays outdoors in a light airy place out of the sun.

LATE SUMMER/AUTUMN

ACONITUM. *Monkshood. A. carmichaelii, to 4', Z3; Cultivars and hybrids. Sun; part shade where summers are hot, but not a plant for the South. Fertile, moist soil. NOTE: All parts are highly poisonous.*

No other plant in the late summer garden offers the rare beauty of the blue and purple monkshoods. It is not to be grown where children play, however, nor cut for a centerpiece where food is eaten, as it is a poisonous plant. Superficially the plants resemble delphinium, but they are more sturdy, contained, and dependable. They have branching racemes of curious hooded flowers, about an inch high, that resemble Roman helmets. They do not transplant well, yet need dividing every several years.

One of the best for cutting is *Aconitum carmichaelii* 'Arendsii', blooming a vibrant blue on four-foot high strong stems. I grow it in the back of the border, flanked by white and pink Japanese anemones and assorted asters, which also make good vase companions. Other good choices are *A.* 'Bressingham Spire', violet-blue, about a foot shorter and requiring no staking; 'Newry Blue', navy blue, blooming slightly earlier than the other two. All hold up well in water for about a week.

Pick after several flowers at the base of the stem have opened. Condition overnight in warm water. Take care in handling, as some people may be sensitive to the sap. Do not let flowers or stems touch open wounds. The green seed heads are also pretty in bouquets; hung upside down to dry, they will turn brown.

ANEMONE. *Anemone, windflower. A. × hybrida (Japanese anemone) to 5'; Z6. Sun or part shade. Moist soil.*

Charming and colorful anemones bloom in spring gardens and woodlands, but as cut-flowers, none excels the taller-growing hybrids known as Japanese anemones, which refresh the garden from late summer until frost. They are tough plants with coarse but handsome basal leaves that look good all summer. They are slow to arise in spring, and slow to take hold, then spread rambunctiously, sending up many tall wandlike flower stalks. The flowers are round, from two to three inches

wide, in loose clusters or solitary, and create an airy effect. They come in singles, semidoubles and doubles, in white and assorted shades of pink.

My first choice among the whites is 'Honorine Jobert', which dates back to 1858; its pristine single blooms are carried on two-foot long stems; two- to three-inch rounded blooms have yellow centers and an impeccable form. Among the pinks, 'September Charm', silvery pink, and 'Queen Charlotte', a clear pink semidouble, are both good. There are cultivars in rose and salmon shades as well.

After they become established, in two to three years, Japanese anemones are rugged, reliable, and pest-resistant; even the five-footers do not need staking, but they do require dividing every several years to curb their spread. They add a dainty touch to mass displays. After petals fall, the round balls that remain on the stems, together with unopened buds, make pretty airy accents in an autumnal mélange of blooms and foliage.

Cut when petals open but centers are still tight. Remove lower leaves and stand the stems in cold water overnight. If stems become soft or decayed, recut them. For drying, cut stems just as flowers open and place in silica gel for a few days, or use the oven method.

ARTEMISIA. *Artemisia, mugwort. A. lactiflora (white mugwort), to 6', Z5. A.*

ludoviciana, *to 3½', Z4. Most artemisias do best in full sun and lean well-drained soil, and will not tolerate hot muggy summers;* A. lactiflora *needs moist heavy soil and some shade.*

Gray-leaved artemisias are attractive foliage plants and make fine additions to fresh and dried arrangements. Their gray, white, and silvery leaves provide textural variety for the garden and bouquets. They serve as foils for strong colors, often softening those that clash. Of many excellent varieties, I would not be without *Artemisia* × 'Powis Castle', with silky filigreed foliage that grows into a three-foot mound, and provides a lacey look to bouquets. *A. ludoviciana* 'Silver Queen' and the slightly taller 'Silver King' are valuable for floral displays and dried wreaths, contributing lovely frosty willow-leaves, and flowering slender plumes of tiny grayish white flowers in late summer; beware of their roots, which will overrun the border unless controlled.

The only artemisia grown for its flowers is the tall-growing *A. lactiflora*, which puts out showy creamy astilbe-like plumes about 18 inches long; it makes an excellent long lasting cut flower, good with yellow daisies and sunflowers, blue salvias, monkshoods, and asters.

Foliage can be picked throughout the summer, but for the longest vase life, pick when mature. The whiter, felted leaves last longer than silky-haired foliage. Put stems into water immediately after cutting. Split woody stems and give them a long drink. Dip ends of soft stems briefly in a few inches of hot water, then allow them to stand in several inches of water overnight. The stems can be cut to any length. To dry hang mature stems upside down. Some varieties will dry well while left standing in an arrangement in water; experiment.

ASTER. *Hardy aster.* A. × frikartii, *to 3', Z5;* A. novae-angliae *(New England aster), to 6', Z3;* A. novi-belgii *(New York aster), to 6', Z4. Sun or bright shade. Well-drained, moderately fertile soil, except New York aster, which prefers moist, fertile soil.*

Of the many first-rate asters for the autumn garden, none deserves more praise than *Aster × frikartii*. It is sturdy and well-branched, yet elegant; fragrant, and at three feet, a nice sized plant. In my garden it blooms from late July to October. I like 'Monch' for its lavender blue daisies with a yellow eye, about three inches

wide, which is charming in bouquets. 'Wonder of Staffa' is similar.

New England and New York asters and their hybrids, also known as Michaelmas daisies, are stately, bold, and tough, showy at the back of borders and also good in meadow gardens and other informal areas. They provide armloads of flowers at a time of year when other plants have slowed. There are many cultivars available. Of the New England asters, my first choice is 'Alma Potschke' with sheets of bright cerise daisies over several weeks; 'Treasurer', which is exceedingly generous with its deep lilac blooms; and 'Harrington's Pink', a late bloomer with clear pink flowers, which should be cut back in late June to prevent legginess and assure more upright stems. Among the New York asters, 'Marie Ballard', an old cultivar, has lovely powder blue blooms; 'Sailor Boy' has the darkest blue flowers.

Cut asters when about three-quarters of the flowers on a stem are open. Split woody ends and dip them in hot water for a few seconds to release air bubbles. Recut soft stems under warm water. Add a tablespoon of sugar to each quart of conditioning water, and give stems a long drink. Before arranging, strip lower leaves from the stems; remove upper ones only as they wilt as they are reported to increase longevity. Smaller daisy heads can be dried in silica gel.

CIMICIFUGA. *Cimicifuga, bugbane.* C. racemosa *(black cohosh) to 8', Z3;*

C. ramosa, *to 7', Z3; C. simplex (Kam-chatka bugbane) to 4', Z4. Morning sun, light shade. Rich moisture-retentive soil on the acidic side; benefits from a mulch of leaf mold.*

Cimicifuga is an outstanding choice for the border, wildflower garden, and house. *Cimicifuga racemosa* blooms in midsummer for a month and is ideal for the back of the border or planted in a wild garden where its spikes of white "fairy candles" can sway in the breeze. Although a giant, its stems are strong and self-supporting. If grown in dry soil in warmer climates, however, its leaves can scorch and turn brown in high summer. Some say that its flowers have a nasty smell, but the scent dissipates after the stalks are conditioned and arranged.

C. ramosa 'Atropurpurea' peaks in September and is the most ornamental variety, with superb, coppery purple leaves and stems; the flower buds are touched with the same coloring, opening to a contrasting cream white. Kamchatka bugbane (*C. simplex*) blooms in October. 'White Pearl' is a compact cultivar to four feet tall. Foot-long graceful spikes densely covered with pearllike florets bloom for several weeks. If not cut, these are followed by decorative green fruits that are useful for cutting.

Cut the stems when about a third of the spike has bloomed. Place stem ends in boiling water for a few seconds; condition in cold water for at least several hours. Cimicifugas make a lovely centerpiece by themselves;

shorten the spikes at the bottom for the height desired. They also add delicate vertical touches to mixed arrangements. To dry, cut when half the florets on a spike are open and buds are fat; dry lengthwise in silica gel in a low oven, which will take about six hours. Hang green seed heads of 'White Pearl' upside down to dry.

CLEMATIS. *Clematis.* Vine. C. × jackmanii *(Jackman), to 12', Z3; C. max-imowicziana (sweet autumn clematis; sometimes offered as* C. paniculata*), to 20', Z5; C. tangutica, to 15', Z5. Various cultivars. Flowering is best in full sun;* C. paniculata *and* jackmanii *hybrids will take some shade; keep roots of all clematis cool. Alkaline, free-draining soil.*

It is in late summer and autumn, when the glut of other flowers has dwindled, that the arching flower-studded stems and tendrils of clematis are most appreciated for arranging.

The vigorous sweet autumn clematis (*C. maximowicziana*) dependably furnishes sheets of lacy white, deliciously fragrant star flowers from August until frost. It is virtually indestructible, and can be cut to the ground in early spring. (Consult a good garden reference book for guidance in growing and pruning clematis; see Bibliography.) Another favorite for cutting is *C. tangutica*, which displays yellow, one-and-a-half-inch bells against silvery green leaves into fall; like many clematis, its blooms are followed by attractive,

feathery seed heads that make lovely accents.

Among the many large-flowered vining clematis with four- to six-inch flowers that are still blooming in September, I would choose purplish blue *C. × jackmanii*; 'Nelly Moser', with rose-pink bars down the center of each pale mauve sepal; 'Niobe' as the best deep red; and 'Duchess of Edinburgh', which is sparkling white with striking yellow stamens.

Cut stems (include some of the woody vine) of the large varieties when sepals begin to unfold, or when more than a quarter of the smaller flowers in a cluster are open. Split woody stem ends, then dip them in boiling water for a few seconds; condition overnight in warm water. The Japanese dip stem ends in pure alcohol for a few hours, then condition them in warm water. Flowers last well from several days to a week. The fluffy white seed heads on some clematis can be sprayed with a light sealant to preserve them for dried arrangements. Dry individual flowers or small sprays in silica gel.

HELIANTHUS. *Perennial sunflower. H. decapetalus to 6', Z4; H. salicifolius (willow-leaf sunflower) to 6', Z3.* **HELIOPSIS.** *False sunflower. H. helianthoides* ssp. *scabra, to 4', Z3. Both generally require sun; ordinary soil. Heliopsis* tolerates heat and drought.

Perennial sunflower and false sunflower are very similar. While they begin to bloom earlier in the season, both continue to produce their fresh bright yellow flowers into fall. Each has showy, daisylike flowers, up to five inches across on long stems, and both are treasured cut flowers. They are incredibly prolific and you can cut freely; actually, regular cutting prolongs their flowering.

Perennial sunflowers, closely allied to the annual sunflower (*Helianthus annuus*), are less refined than false sunflower and some are highly invasive and should be carefully placed. My favorite is the bushy willow-leaf *H. salicifolius,* six feet tall and covered with zillions of two-inch sunny blooms with contrasting purplish brown disks. For larger flowers, both *H. decapetalus* 'Loddon Gold' and 'Flore Pleno' are good doubles with four-inch-wide gold and bright yellow flowers respectively.

The best cultivars of *H. helianthoides* ssp. *scabra* include the double-flowered 'Golden Greenheart', delightful with yellow ray flowers surrounding a bright green disc that fades as the bloom matures. 'Karat'

has large single blooms in clear yellow. Orange-flowered 'Summer Sun' is the best for southern gardens.

Cut sunflowers when the ray flowers turn out, revealing their tight centers. Remove lower and unnecessary foliage and condition in cool water before arranging. They are stunning alone, with white daisies, or with fall foliage and berries. Allow seed heads to dry on the plant for winter use indoors. Protect from birds as they ripen with nylon mesh or torn pantyhose.

HYDRANGEA. Shrub. Hydrangea paniculata *'Grandiflora' (peegee hydrangea), to 15', Z3. Sun or light shade. Moist, rich soil.*

For large arrangements of bulk and beauty, I am fond of *Hydrangea paniculata* 'Grandiflora', known as peegee hydrangea, which is also the best hydrangea for drying. It grows as a single-stemmed small tree, and blooms in late summer with enormous pan-

icles of white flowers on arching stems; the flower trusses are conical, about a foot and a half long, and very dramatic. They gradually change colors to cream, old-rose, and bronze, as the foliage itself turns to mellow yellow; after they succumb to frost, they turn brown. Half a dozen long stems poked through chicken wire in a tall container can decorate the fireplace until you tire of them, first as fresh flowers, then as a dried display; just allow the stems to dry naturally in a few inches of water.

To cut, select flower heads that are fully open and have been in bloom for several days; cut stems flush with a main branch, or on long branches, to the length you want. Remove most of the foliage, which wilts quickly after it is arranged. Split stems and dunk them in an inch or so of boiling water for a few seconds before conditioning them in cold water up to their necks. If the blooms seem wilted, immerse them in cold water until they are crisp. The flower heads also can be snipped or pulled apart to create any shape or size you want.

To dry, select flower panicles at the desired color stage, but after the flowers are mature and before they are touched by hard frost, which rots them. Hang the flower heads upside down to dry. Or dry them standing up in a container in a few inches of water in a warm place. Either way, do not allow their heads to touch. By treating the stems in glycerin, the flower heads will turn an attractive satiny brown.

PHLOX. *Phlox.* P. paniculata *(garden or border phlox), to 5', Z3. Full sun for best flowering. Moist soil enriched with decayed organic matter.*

These handsome plants are usually thought of as the mainstay of the midsummer border, but many continue to bloom into fall; indeed, a few have been bred to bloom as late as September when the garden is often in need of their perky splotches of color. Cultivars feature pyramidal clusters of showy flowers in colors ranging from pure white through fiery crimson and rich purple, but no blue or yellow; often there is an eye of a darker or lighter zone in the center.

'Bright Eyes', clear pink with a deeper pink eye, grows to a little less than three feet and is an excellent midborder plant and a dependable cut flower, producing medium-size trusses that are not too heavy-looking in arrangements. It belongs to the Symons-Jeune strain of phlox, which is especially long blooming

and said to be mildew-resistant, which it has so far proved to be in my garden. 'Mount Fujiyamo', among the latest to bloom, puts out large heads of snow-white flowers in September. 'Orange Perfection' is the best of the salmon and orange shades and I like 'Starfire' for a good cherry red. Select plants when they are in bloom at the nursery to be sure of getting the colors you want. Cut off several inches from their tops about late July to encourage side shoots that will also flower.

Pick phlox when one-quarter to one-half of the panicles are open and put them in water immediately; once they flag they cannot be resuscitated. Split thick stems and condition in warm water. Pick off withered blossoms daily to encourage new buds to open and keep the flower head looking fresh. Phlox are magnificent in large arrangements; mass them in a large basket or wooden bowl. Phlox does not dry well.

SEDUM. *Sedum, stonecrop.* S. 'Autumn Joy', *to 2', Z3;* S. telephium *(great stonecrop), to 2', Z3;* S. 'Vera Jameson', *to 1', Z3. Will take full sun in the North; afternoon shade in the South. Lean, well-drained soil. Drought-resistant.*

There are many sedums, but only a handful are tall enough to be useful in the border and for cutting. *Sedum* 'Autumn Joy' is the most remarkable and dependable. Its sturdy, straight stems put it head and shoulders above most sedums, which tend to sprawl, and adds to its superiority as

a cut flower. It is an easy perennial to grow; even when not in bloom its succulent gray-green leaves are attractive. Flowering begins about August in my garden, with broccolilike clusters of buds slowly unfolding to showy domes of flattish flower heads; these turn from rose-pink to russet as the flowers age, and finally to dark mahogany seed heads. It is attractive in all stages of this metamorphosis. The cut flower heads will last from seven to ten days.

Another tall sedum, *S. telephium* 'Atropurpureum', is prized for its vivid purple foliage and dark red flattish flower clusters, which add distinction to arrangements. One of the few good shorter sedums is *S.* 'Vera Jameson'—purple foliage with a gray blush and pretty dusky pink flower clusters which are good in smaller bouquets.

Cut sedums when the clusters are half in flower; they will continue to open in water. Condition in cold water for several hours. Foliage can be picked throughout the growing season for textural accents. Pick stems with dense close-growing leaves and immerse them in cold water for half an hour. They will last from two to three weeks. Use sedums in masses, as focal points, to give visual weight at the base of arrangements, and as fillers. Flower clusters of most sedums do not dry successfully. Hang the rich brown seed heads of 'Autumn Joy' upside down to dry.

VIBURNUM. Shrub. *V. dilatatum (linden viburnum), to 10', Z5. Sun, part shade. Moist soil on the acid side.*

Viburnums are marvelous ornamental shrubs that capture the mood of the seasons, bursting with flowering branches in spring and laden with berries in fall, while their foliage takes on fiery hues. For autumn interest in the garden that also offers cut branches for the house, the linden viburnum ranks at the

top. It puts out the best berry (botanically, the fruit is a "drupe") display and its yellow, orange, and red leaves last a surprising long time in water—several days—compared with most autumn foliage. The astonishing five-inch clusters of shiny rich red berries begin to appear against the autumn-tinted foliage in September, and linger into December. 'Iroquois' is a good selection

for its heavy textured foliage, turning to maroon, and an abundant crop of large berries. The berries of 'Erie' turn to coral and pink after frost, and 'Catskill' is a dwarf that grows to five feet in 13 years, with dark red berries and good leaf color in autumn.

Cut branches when the berries or foliage has reached the desired stage or color. Cut selectively to enhance the shape of the shrub so that no further pruning will be needed. Slit or hammer the stems and condition for several hours in deep water. The colored leaves and berries can be used in fresh or dried arrangements with other foliage and flowers to give background structure and for autumn accents. Branches with autumn foliage will not last long out of water in dried displays; stand them in individual smaller containers with water and place them among the dried stems. The green foliage preserves well in glycerin.

APPENDIXES

PLANT LISTS

Woody Plants

Abelia ×grandiflora, glossy abelia; *shrub* to 6', z6. Sun; moist, acidic soil with good drainage. Funnel-shaped flowers, white-and-pink, from June through frost. Good glossy foliage, turns bronze-red in fall. *Abelia* 'Edward Goucher' has darker pink flowers.

Amelanchier arborea, downy serviceberry, shadbush; multistemmed *shrub* or small *tree* to 25', z4. Sun, part shade; moist acidic soil. White, pendant flower clusters on slender stems with tender foliage, gray underneath. Late April blooming, red berries turn to purple in June. Good fall foliage color. Many cultivars. 'Autumn Sunset' has rich orange foliage in fall. May be cut for forcing in late January.

Buddleia alternifolia 'Argentea', fountain butterfly bush; *shrub* to 15', z5. Sun; well-drained soil. Blooms in late May, showy clusters of dark lilac flowers on slender stems. Silvery attractive foliage.

Caryopteris × clandonensis, bluebeard, blue spirea; *shrub* to 3', z6. Sun; average soil with good drainage. Delicate shrub with slender branches, silvery green foliage and tiered spikes of blue fringed flowers from August until frost. 'Blue Mist' is a powdery blue; 'Heavenly Blue' is a strong violet; 'Dark Knight' is purple-blue. Good filler and complement to late-blooming annuals and perennials. Treat as a herbaceous perennial and cut back in late winter.

Celastrus scandens, American bittersweet; *vine* to about 20', z3. Sun; any soil will do. Need male and female plants to set fruit. Yellow-orange fruit, crimson seed pods, in October. Good in dried arrangements. Pick before the outer shells have opened.

Chaenomeles speciosa, common flowering quince; *shrub* to 10', z4. Sun, part shade; any soil. White to red flowers in spring. 'Cameo' is a double apricot; 'Jet Trail' is white; 'Texas Scarlet' is red. Good for forcing in February. Dry in silica gel.

Clematis, clematis, species, cultivars, hybrids; *vine* to 20', z3. Sun; moist soil, shaded roots. *C. montana*, anemone clematis: May-June flowering—'Grandiflora' has three-inch white blooms; 'Elizabeth' has large, pink fragrant blooms. *C. × jackmanii* hybrids: June flowering—'Henryi' has five-inch creamy white flowers with dark stamens; 'Ramona' has lavender-blue flowers with dark anthers. July-August flowering: 'Hagley Hybrid' has shell-pink flowers with brown anthers; 'Perle d'Azur' is sky blue; 'Gipsy Queen' is a rich violet-purple. Dry in sand or silica gel. Pick ornamental feathery seed heads before they are mature.

Clethra alnifolia, summersweet; *shrub* to 8', z3. Sun or shade; moist, acid organic soil. White, very fragrant small flowers on six-inch long panicles in July and August. 'Pink Spires' has rose buds that open to soft pink.

Cornus florida, flowering dogwood; *tree* to 20', z5. Sun, part shade; moist but well-drained acidic soil enriched with organic matter. Showy white "flowers" (white bracts with small true flowers at the center), about four inches across in April and May. Ornamental glossy red fruit in October, handsome foliage with excellent reddish purple fall color. Forces easily; dry flowers and foliage. Many cultivars. 'American Beauty Red' has deep red bracts. 'Cloud 9' has profuse showy white bracts. 'Red Cloud' has pink bracts.

Cornus kousa, kousa or Chinese dogwood; *tree* to 30', z5. Sun; acidic well-drained sandy soil enriched with organic matter. In June creamy white or pinkish bracts bloom above the foliage along the branches, lasting six weeks or longer. Ornamental fruit resembles large raspberries in August; foliage for autumn color. 'Rosabella', a cultivar of *C. k.* var. *chinesis*, is rose pink. 'Milky Way' is an extremely floriferous, compact form for small landscapes.

Cotinus coggygria, smoke bush; *shrub* or small *tree* to 15', z5. Sun; not fussy but does best in well-drained loamy soils. Hazes of hairy eight-inch-long panicles of tiny yellowish flowers from June through August; the hairs produce a smoky pink or purple effect. Good for fresh and dried arrangements. Useful red or purple foliage, more brilliant in fall. 'Royal Purple' is the darkest purple-leaved cultivar.

Cotoneaster conspicuus, wintergreen cotoneaster; evergreen, spreading *shrub* to 4', z6. Sun; adapts to many soils, but with good drainage. Small white flowers, one-half inch in diameter, in early June, attractive tiny glossy leaves (gray underneath), good fruiting shrub with dark red berries that persist and are useful in winter displays. Offers foliage for arrangements all year.

Cytisus × *praecox*, Warminster broom; *shrub* to 10', z5. Sun; adaptable but prefers sandy soil. Abundant small pea-shaped flowers in May grow along slender bristly stems. 'Albus' is white flowering; 'Canary Bird' is yellow. 'Hollandia' is smaller, to four feet, with salmon-pink flowers. Foliage is good for linear effects. Air-dry green branches.

Daphne × *burkwoodii*, Burkwood daphne. Pretty, small *shrub* to 4', z4. Sun to light shade; neutral sandy but moist soil. May blooming with small whitish pink blossoms in dense clusters, about two inches across, and leaves about an inch long. Sweetly fragrant. 'Somerset' has semievergreen foliage. 'Carol Mackie' has elegant cream-edged leaf margins and light pink flowers, to three feet, useful for cutting even when not in flower.

Exochorda racemosa, common pearlbush; *shrub* to 15', z4. Sun or part shade; acidic, loamy soil. Spectacular flowering with small white flowers in five-inch-long sprays covering the ends of stems beginning in late April or early May for two weeks. Unopened buds look like white pearls. Rich brown seed capsules in autumn.

Fothergilla major, large fothergilla; *shrub* to 10', z4. Sun, part shade in hot areas; acidic soil. Short two-inch fragrant white bottlebrush spikes in April and early May. Good for forcing. Brilliant fall leaf colors in yellow, orange, and scarlet.

Hydrangea arborescens, smooth hydrangea; *shrub* to 5', z3. Sun or part shade; rich, moist but well-drained soil. In June large apple-green flower heads, six inches or more in diameter, turn white and last several weeks before turning brown. 'Annabelle' bears symmetrical upright flower heads, up to a foot

across. Prune in late fall or early spring. Good for large-scale arrangements, or edit flowers by separating into smaller sections. Air-dry by hanging, or standing in a vase with an inch or two of water.

H. macrophylla, bigleaf, or mophead hydrangea; *shrub* to 6', z6. Part shade, or sun if soil is kept moist; pH of the soil affects flower color of some cultivars, with an acidic range of 5.0 to 5.5 producing blue flowers, and 6.0 to 6.5 resulting in pink flowers. Flowers appear in July and August and come in two kinds: large globes of white, pink, red, or blue flowers of the hortensias; and the broad, flat-topped lacecaps, with a central ring of florets surrounded by a showy outer ring. *H. macrophylla* blooms on old wood and should only be pruned right after flowering. Many cultivars for both fresh and dried cut flowers.

Kolkwitzia amabilis, beauty bush; *shrub* to 10', z4. Full sun, ordinary garden soil. Lovely bell-shaped flowers, shell pink with a yellow throat in showy clusters on arching branches. 'Pink Cloud' has clear pink flowers, green foliage turning light orange in fall. Attractive seed capsules for dried arrangements.

Leucothoe fontanesiana, drooping leucothoe, fetterbush; evergreen *shrub* to 6', z5. Part shade to full shade, or sun in moist soil; rich, acidic, moist soil. White drooping flower clusters about three inches long; fragrant. Lustrous leaves good year-round background foliage in arrangements.

Lonicera fragrantissima, winter honeysuckle; *shrub* to 10', z4. Sun, part shade, adaptable, but prefers loamy, moist soil. Small, creamy, lemon-scented flowers in late March, for several weeks. Versatile on the landscape, good for forcing; adds fragrance and blooms to early bouquets.

L. × *heckrotti*, everblooming or gold-flame honeysuckle; woody *vine* to 20', z5. Sun, part shade; adaptable to various soils. Carmine buds open to fragrant flowers, yellow inside, outside changing to pink with age. Long-lasting, sporadic blooms until fall. Flowers can be forced.

L. tatarica, tatarian honeysuckle; *shrub* to 12', z4. Sun, part shade, adaptable to various soils. Pink to white flowers in May, red berries throughout summer. 'Parvifolia' has large white flowers. 'Hack's Red' is deep purplish red. 'Lutea' has pink flowers, yellow fruit.

Malus, flowering crab apple; ornamental, deciduous small *trees* and *shrubs*, to 25', variable hardiness—many to z4, some to z5. Sun, adaptable to many soils. Many types with diverse foliage, blossoms, and fruits are available. Many are susceptible to various diseases; seek advice from local nurseries to select cultivars that perform well in your area. Cultivars, among many others, that are disease resistant include 'Angel Choir', with pale pink buds opening to double white flowers, red fruit; 'Cardinal's Robes', orange-red buds opening to bright red, red fruit; 'Thundercloud', delicate rose flowers, red-purple fruit. Cut branches for forcing, to mix with spring bulbs; dry blossoms in sand or silica gel.

Paeonia suffruticosa hybrids, tree peony; *shrub* to 6', z5. Full sun, but will grow in light shade; loamy, well-drained neutral soil. Magnificent silky blooms, to ten inches across, in early spring before herbaceous peonies bloom. Modern cultivars bloom for four weeks, with up to 70 blooms on a mature plant. Chinese, Japanese, and other hybrids offer flowers in shades of pink, red, yellow, and purple. 'Godaishu' is semidouble white with a gold center; 'Hatsi Garashu' is single dark red with a yellow center; 'Age of Gold' is double with creamy gold anthers and fragrant. Cut sparingly to maintain the shrub's vigor. Dry blooms in silica gel. Pick seed heads while still green and hang upside down to dry. Preserve leaves in glycerin for winter arrangements.

Philadelphus, mock orange, cultivars and hybrids; *shrub* to 12', z4. Full sun to light shade; moist, well-drained soil enriched with organic matter. White fragrant inch-and-a-half-long flowers, in clusters on arching branches in May to early June. Double-flowered varieties last longer (five days to a week) than single, which tend to shatter. 'Frosty Morn' is a very fragrant double, to five feet. 'Dwarf Snowflake' is a very fragrant double, to four feet. Cut in mid-March for forcing. For arrangements, remove most of the foliage. Short sprays of double-flowered varieties are better candidates for drying in sand than singles; variable success.

Pieris japonica, Japanese pieris (also mistakenly called andromeda); evergreen *shrub* to 12', spread of 8', z5. Sun, part shade; acidic well-drained soil is best. Pendant urn-shaped flower panicles, six inches long, in March and April. New foliage is bronze, turning to glossy green. Many cultivars. 'Mountain Fire' has white flowers; spring foliage is fiery red. 'Coleman' is pink flowered. Forced flowers last over a week. Foliage can be cut year-round.

Prunus cerasifera 'Thundercloud', thundercloud plum; *tree* to 25', z5. Full sun for best foliage color, ordinary soil. Single fragrant pink flowers open around early April before the leaves, which have the deepest color of all purple plums. Cut after buds begin to swell, or six weeks ahead of normal blooming for forcing. Purple foliage is attractive in arrangements.

Pyracantha coccinea, scarlet firethorn; semievergreen to evergreen *shrub* to 18', good for espaliers on trellises; z5. Full sun, part shade; acidic to neutral soil. Showy clusters of tiny, creamy white flowers appear along ends of stems in late May; ornamental orange-red berries appear in fall. Cultivars feature yellow, orange, or red fruit. Dry berried branches upright in an inch or two of water for use in winter arrangements.

Spiraea × *bumalda,* bumald spirea; low *shrub* to 3' high and 5' wide, z3. Sun; adaptable to many soils except very wet. Deep-pink flat-topped flower clusters, to six inches in diameter, in late May and June. If blooms are removed, new growth and additional flowers result. 'Anthony Waterer' grows to four feet with carmine-pink flowers. 'Goldflame' has pink flowers and spectacular foliage for cutting and garden effect, beginning as russet or bronze in spring, turning to yellow and finally green; this same color pattern is reversed in fall.

S. prunifolia, bridalwreath spirea; *shrub* to 9', z4. Full sun; tolerant of many soils. Long-lasting, white, double, buttonlike flowers on arching branches in early May. Glossy green foliage in summer, orangy red in fall.

S. × *vanhouttei,* vanhoutte spirea; vase-shaped, arching *shrub* to 8', z3. Sun; ordinary soil. A taller, earlier-blooming shrub than *S.* × *bumalda,* with myriad white florets in dainty clusters about an inch and a half across along arching branches in late April. Cut for forcing in March after buds begin to swell. Flowers shed some, but they are lovely in any case.

Symplocos paniculata, sapphireberry; large *shrub* or small *tree* to 20', z4. Full sun; no particular soil needs except good drainage. Three-inch-long panicles of many fragrant small white blossoms come out in early June. Branches become heavy with bright blue berrylike fruit in September-October; pick before birds strip branches.

Viburnum × *burkwoodii,* Burkwood viburnum; *shrub* to 10', z4. Sun, well-drained but moist, slightly acidic soil enriched with organic matter. Pink buds open to white round flower clusters, about three inches across in April. Spicy fragrance. Red to black berries in fall. Highly ornamental as cut flowering branches in spring, and berried branches with colorful foliage in fall. 'Mohawk', to eight feet, has brilliant red flower buds opening to white petals blotched in red on the reverse; very fragrant; leaves turn wine red in fall.

Weigela florida, old-fashioned weigela; *shrub* to 9', z4. Full sun; moist soil. Many cultivars available with white, pink, or red tubular flowers, about an inch and a half long, in profusion on arching branches in late May and June. 'Mont Blanc' has large white fragrant flowers. 'Eva Rathke', a compact shrub, has bright red flowers with yellow anthers. 'Variegata' has deep rose flowers and variegated leaves in cream or white. Myriad blooms and color override the tendency of the flowers to shatter.

Wisteria floribunda, Japanese wisteria; *vine* to over 30', z4. Sun; moist, loamy soil. Small, fragrant flowers in long slender racemes about 20 inches long bloom in early May before leaves appear. Cultivar flowers range from white to dark purple. 'Ivory Tower' is fragrant white; 'Rosea' is pale rose with purple-tipped petals; 'Royal Purple' is violet-purple. Hang to dry. Seedpods are good in dried bouquets.

Annuals

For best flowering, give the following annuals plenty of sun. Most will grow well in average garden soil enriched with composted organic matter.

Amaranthus caudatus, love-lies-bleeding. Cut when about three-fourths of the dark-red or golden florets on long tassels are open for best color. Remove unnecessary foliage, split stems, condition overnight in deep warm water. Good for large, dramatic arrangements. Red-leaved form is most attractive. May be hung to dry; color fades and will eventually turn brown.

Ammi majus, white lace flower. Fernlike leaves and flat-topped flower clusters, like Queen Anne's lace. (Make sequenced sowings, about two weeks apart, for a longer period of picking.) Pick when about half the florets in a cluster are open. Condition overnight in warm water to start. Romantic, lacy effect, good in June bridal bouquets if seeds are begun early indoors.

Antirrhinum majus, snapdragon. Cut when half the flower spike is in flower. Condition overnight, beginning with hot water to start. Add one tablespoon sugar or flower preservative to one quart of conditioning water. Adds fluffy tapering vertical lines to bouquets. Dries well in sand or silica gel.

Bupleurum rotundifolium, thoroughwax. (Easily grown from seed.) Cut sprays when chartreuse flowers, similar to those of euphorbia, begin to appear against eucalyptuslike foliage. Condition in room-temperature water for several hours. Good filler. Lightly branched flower heads will animate an arrangement.

Calendula officinalis, pot marigold. Cut just before flowers open fully. Recut stems under water. Add one teaspoon bleach to each quart of conditioning water to retard bacterial growth. Dry flowers in silica gel; remove foliage first.

Callistephus chinensis, China aster. Blooms come in shades of purple, blue, pink, and white. Cut just before blooms open. Recut stems under water and condition overnight, adding one tablespoon of sugar for each quart of water. Will last from ten days to two weeks.

Not recommended for drying, as it shatters.

Campanula medium, Canterbury bell, *biennial.* Cup-and-saucer-shaped blooms in white, pink, and blue. Cut when several blooms on a stalk have opened. Split and sear stem ends, then condition overnight in hot water to start. If blooms flag prematurely, recut and recondition the same way. Dry flowers in silica gel; takes three to four days.

Celosia spp., cockscomb. Flowers from the comb or crested kinds may be cut at any stage. Wide range of heights and colors in white, yellow, red, and purple and shades in between. Colors become richer in cool weather. Cut plume or feather types when they are fully open, as undeveloped flowers will not hold. Remove unnecessary foliage, split stems, and condition overnight. Both crested and plume celosia may be hung to dry.

Centaurea cyanus, bachelor's-button, cornflower. Blue, pink, red, and white. Will bloom all summer. Cut when flowers are freshly open; buds will not open in water. Condition overnight in tepid water. Cut flowers will last five to seven days.

Clarkia spp., godetia, satin flower. Flowers profusely, even in part shade. Comes in a wide range of colors, with satiny or frilly petals. Good as a filler flower. Cut after several blooms have opened. Split stems and condition overnight. Buds will continue to open.

Cleome hasslerana, spider flower. Pink, red, white. Large globular flower heads give a light, airy effect. (Self-seeding, can become invasive.) Cut when flower cluster is half open. Will wilt initially, but will revive during conditioning. Split stems, condition in warm water overnight.

Cobaea scandens, cup-and-saucer vine (cathedral bells). Showy velvet blue

flowers. Can climb 10 to 15 feet. Cut curving branches with mix of flowers and buds. Condition overnight in warm water. Good trailer over edge of container.

Consolida ambigua, annual larkspur. White, pink, blue, lavender. Blooms all summer. Cut when half the spike is in bloom; plump buds will continue to open in water. Condition overnight in tepid water. Remove spent flowers. Useful upright form in bouquets. To dry, pick when flower spike is almost entirely open; dry in silica gel for best results; air-dry also, but shrinkage will occur.

Cosmos spp., cosmos. White, pink, red, brilliant orange. Cut sprays with open blooms and tight centers; snip off mature flowers. Condition in deep cold water overnight. Delicate effect, or mass for a heavier look.

Eschscholzia californica, California poppy. (Sow seeds outdoors where they are to bloom; most poppies resent transplanting.) Free-blooming single or double blooms over a long period in white, pink, yellow, salmon, orange, cerise, and carmine. Cut stems just before flowers open and condition overnight. Will last several days.

Eustoma grandiflorum, lisianthus, prairie gentian. A half-hardy perennial in the South; grown as an annual north of Washington, D.C. Showy single or double flowers similar to roses and tulips, three inches across, on foot-and-a-half stems. Elegant blue-gray foliage. Color range is white, pink, red, blue, purple, yellow, and bicolors. Best to buy plants; difficult to grow from seeds, which must be started indoors in January. Cut when the flower at the top of each stem is about half open and buds farther down are mature. Condition for a few hours in warm water. Flowers last remarkably long—about two weeks, even longer with floral preservative in vase water. The fragile flowers are usually not dried; you may wish to experiment.

Gaillardia spp., blanket flower. Cut when blooms are open but centers still tight. Condition overnight. Daisylike flowers. Double varieties are longer lasting when cut than singles. Bicolored in shades of yellow, orange, and red. Hang upside down to dry.

Helianthus annuus, annual sunflower. Double forms with sunflowers four to six inches across are most practical for home arrangements. Colors range from creamy white through yellow, rose, orange, red, copper, and bicolors with dark disks at center. Cut when flower face is open but the center still tight. When branches are multiflowered, select stems with a few freshly opened flower heads. Remove unnecessary foliage and slit stem ends about an inch high. Condition at least overnight in warm water to start; condition large heads longer. Some stems may need support for heavy flower heads; do this by inserting heavy wire through stem from flower head down. Air-dry seed heads; they are attractive with or without seeds.

Lathyrus odoratus, sweet pea. Lovely colors, delicate form, and heavenly fragrance; a must. Plants need rich soil, cool, moist conditions, some support, and regular cutting. (Use pea sticks to support short varieties.) Cut when almost all the flowers on a slender stem are open. Add a floral preservative or one tablespoon of sugar to each quart of warm conditioning water; allow stems to stand in the water overnight. Dry blossoms in silica gel.

Lavatera trimestris, tree mallow. Hollyhocklike single flowers in white, satiny pink, and rose. Gather when at least one flower of each cluster has blossomed; buds will continue to open in water. Remove some of the bushy foliage. Split stems; condition overnight in warm water to start.

Matthiola spp., stock. Wide range of colors, very fragrant. Needs cool weather for bud formation. Cut when about half the flower spike is open, split stems, and condition in cold water. If water is highly alkaline, add a few drops of citric acid (obtainable at drugstores).

Molucella laevis, bells-of-Ireland, shell flower. Unusual, showy apple-green "shells," or calyxes, with a tiny central eye surround the stems in whorls; superior as a fresh or dried flower, but must be started from seed, as it is not carried by most nurseries. Flower spikes can be picked in all stages of growth. Strip off leaves and condition in warm water overnight; stems take on natural curves. Will last up to a week. Preserve by standing stems in a solution of glycerin and water for several days. Stems and flower shells will stay supple over many months; shells turn a parchment color.

Nicotiana spp., flowering tobacco. NOTE: All species contain poisonous alkaloids. Fragrant nodding trumpet flowers in white, pink, red, and green, ranging in scale from the dainty flowers of *N. langsdorffii* to the large, dramatic clusters of *N. sylvestris;* plants are from one and a half feet to five feet tall. Blossoms on some species close in midday sun. Cut stems after several blossoms on the branched stem have opened. Condition overnight in warm water. Buds will continue to develop and open for a week of bloom. Remove spent blossoms daily.

Nigella damascena, love-in-a-mist. Feathery foliage and pretty bracts surround flowers. Flowers are white, pink, or shades of blue. For long-season cutting, make about three sowings at three-week intervals. Cut after central flower on a stem has opened. Condition in warm water for several hours. Flowers benefit from the addition of a floral preservative or one tablespoon of sugar for each quart of vase water and will last about a week. Attractive

balloonlike seedpods can be cut in various stages for fresh or dried arrangements. Pick seedpods when still green, but mature, and hang to dry.

Papaver rhoeas, Shirley poppy and cultivars, single and double forms. Papery petals come in soft and bright colors, some in blended tones with golden stamens. Carefully conditioned, the showy flowers should last several days. Pick when buds begin to unfold. Sear stem ends over a hot flame or in boiling water for about ten seconds; condition in cold water overnight.

Petunia × *hybrida,* petunia hybrids. Doubles with long stems and large flowers last longest as cut flowers. Cut freshly opened blossoms from a stem just above a branching point. Strip off leaves below waterline. Blossoms and foliage may wilt after cutting, but will revive during conditioning. Add a tablespoon of sugar per quart of conditioning water; condition overnight. Add a teaspoon of bleach to vase water to retard bacterial growth.

Ricinus communis, castor bean. NOTE: Seeds are highly poisonous to animals and people if ingested. Exotic plant growing to ten feet. Dramatic lobed leaves, useful flower and seed panicles. Dark red variety is best. Cut the sprays of tiny creamy flowers when half the spike has blossomed. Split stems and condition overnight in warm water. Will last more than a week in an arrangement. Foliage and fruits may be cut at various stages. Submerge flowers or fruits in cold water for several hours until crisp. Foliage can last three weeks or longer. (Not a garden center offering; easily grown from seed, but not where children or pets may reach them.)

Rudbeckia hirta, common black-eyed Susan, grown as an annual. Long-lasting vase life, up to two weeks with floral preservative added. Cut as for all daisies, when petals are open and disks are still tight. Condition in tepid water overnight. Foliage wilts before flowers; snip it off and replace with other greenery. To dry, place flower heads down in sand.

Salvia farinacea, mealy-cup sage. Long spikes of small blue or silver-white tubular flowers on two-foot stems, with attractive gray-green foliage. 'Victoria' has rich violet-blue spikes, excellent for cutting and drying. Cut when no more than half the spike has opened and condition for several hours in warm water to start. Either hang to dry or cover in silica gel.

S. horminium 'Claryssa', sage. Blue, pink, and white showy papery bracts on foot-and-a-half stems; excellent in fresh and dried arrangements. Cut when about half the spiky raceme has opened and dip stem ends in about an inch of hot water; condition in deep water for several hours. Hang stems upside down to air-dry.

Scabiosa atropurpurea, pincushion flower. Fluffy, round blossoms in white and shades of blue and red, to mahogany, with many double petals and numerous protruding white or yellow stamens. Taller kinds are best for cutting. Cut when blooms begin to open; split stems and condition overnight. Buds and immature green seedpods are also appealing in bouquets.

Tagetes spp., marigold. Great diversity in heights, sizes, and flower forms. Flowers come in many shades and combinations of yellow, orange, red, and white. Cut when petals are beginning to open but centers are still tight. Remove the bottom leaves, which rot quickly in water. Recut stems under water and condition in cold water overnight. When handling marigolds, the oil glands in the foliage emit a scent that is distasteful to some people. After the

flowers are arranged, the odor disappears. Pick only mature flowers for drying and place face up in sand or silica gel.

Tithonia rotundifolia, Mexican sunflower. Velvety dahlialike flowers of a rich red-orange, some three inches across. Handsome soft foliage also lasts well when cut. Cut freshly opened flowers. Condition overnight in warm water.

Tropaeolum majus and hybrids, nasturtium. Colors range from cream through shades of yellow and red, single and double flowers. Cut flowers when freshly opened, include plump buds. Split stems; condition overnight in cold water. Flowers are light sensitive and will turn toward light. Blossoms are often used to garnish salads. Foliage is attractive; that of 'Alaska' is variegated. When foliage is used alone, condition by standing stems in warm water until turgid.

Verbena bonariensis, verbena. Short-lived perennial grown as an annual. Wiry stems with scattered clusters of lavender flowers on strong stalks. Cut when half the flower clusters on a stalk are open. Split stems; condition overnight in warm water. Adds a light character to bouquets. Outlasts most bouquets, and can be reused. Hang flower heads upside down to dry.

Zinnia elegans, zinnia. (If growing from seed rather than transplants, make a second sowing about mid-June for late-summer flowers. Look for mildew-resistant varieties.) A great variety of heights, sizes, flower forms, and colors, including green, but no blues. Choose open flowers with tight centers; buds do not develop well after cutting. Remove unnecessary foliage and all leaves below water line. Condition overnight in cold water. Sand is the best medium for drying zinnias to maintain their natural appearance. Pick

flower heads when fully opened for best results.

Perennials

Anthemis tinctoria, golden marguerite; to 3', z3. Sun; dry, slightly alkaline soil. Lemon-yellow daisylike flowers from one to two inches across. 'Kelwayi' has parsleylike foliage with a touch of gray and blooms from June through August. Cut stems after a few flowers in a spray have opened; condition in room-temperature water. Will last a week or more. Dry in sand or silica gel.

Asclepias tuberosa, butterfly weed; to 2½', z3. Sun; sandy soil with good drainage. 'Gay Butterflies' produces small tight clusters of tiny flowers on stout stems in hot reds, oranges, and yellows in summer. Pick when at least one-fourth of the florets in a flower head have opened. Sear over a flame or dip in boiling water for about ten seconds; then condition in hot water to start and let stand overnight in deep water. Dry flowers in silica gel. Collect their spiked seedpods from August on for dried arrangements.

Astrantia major, masterwort; to 2', z4. Will take part shade; moist, rich soil. Rounded blossoms of small pincushion florets collared by stiff papery bracts in off-white stained with green or pink. One or two blooms are produced at the ends of slender foot-long wiry stems. 'Rose Symphony' is a pretty pink. *A.m.* ssp. *involucrata* 'Shaggy' has large-toothed bracts. Pick when bracts have fully opened but centers are still fresh. No special conditioning is needed for flowers to last about a week. Treated in glycerine, blossoms turn tawny and are lovely in dried arrangements or wreaths. May also be air-dried; strip off leaves first.

Baptisia australis, blue false indigo; to 4', z3. Sun or part shade; likes somewhat acid soil, tolerates drought. Good deep-blue one-inch flowers on spiky racemes about a foot long and pretty bluish green foliage. Blooms in early summer, followed by attractive pealike pods that turn from green to metallic gray. Flowers, foliage, and seedpods are all useful for arrangements. Cut when about half the flowers on a stem are open; condition in cold water. Seedpods may be cut at the green stage, or after they have turned gray. Leaves preserved in glycerin turn blue.

Bergenia cordifolia, heart-leaved bergenia; to 2', z3. Sun or part shade; not fussy about soil. Dense flower heads of waxy half-inch flowers grow in clusters at the ends of foot-long fleshy stems from April until June. Bold, paddle-shaped leaves, turning bronze-red in autumn, are also valuable for arranging. Condition flowers for several hours in cold water. Submerge foliage in water for a few hours before using; will last about a month in water, or store leaves in a plastic bag in the refrigerator until needed. Leaves turn burgundy-purple when treated with glycerin.

Crocosmia masonorum, crocosmia or montbretia; to 3', z5. Sun, but will tolerate part shade; well-drained, but moist, soil. Bulbous plants with angled sprays of flowers in brilliant shades of red. Flowers are held on strong, wiry, three-foot stems above bright green ribbed leaves similar to those of flowers; 'Firebird' has rich, orange-flame flowers. Cut when a third of the flowers in a spray are open. Give the flower stems a deep drink before arranging; they will last several days to a week. Foliage may be cut, but leave enough behind for the plant to restore itself. Dried seedpods are good for winter arrangements.

Dahlia hybrids, dahlia; to 6', z8; in cooler zones, treat as a tender perennial by lifting tubers and storing over winter. Sun; porous, enriched, moist soil. Available in many colors (except blue) and various flower forms such as cactus, pompon, single, anemone, peony-flowered, decorative, and others. Flower heads range from a few inches up to dinner-plate size, bloom in late summer and autumn. 'Bishop of Llandaff' has blood-red flowers and purplish foliage. 'Park Princess' has tightly rolled cactuslike petals in blended shades of yellow-apricot-rose. Cut flowers when they begin to open; dip stem ends in an inch or two of boiling water for a few seconds, remove foliage, and stand in deep warm water for several hours. Add a teaspoon of bleach to vase water to deter bacteria. For large blooms, float one or two in shallow water in a bowl. Small and pompon shapes dry well in silica gel.

Dendranthema × grandiflorum (formerly *Chrysanthemum × morifolium*), hardy garden chrysanthemum; to 3', z5. Sun; well-drained, slightly acid soil, enriched with compost. Hundreds of cultivars are available in spidery, quilled, pompons, and other shapes, but are not always hardy in the Northeast. Reliable Korean hybrids flower from September until frost, with numerous single and semi-double daisy blooms, to three inches across, in white, yellow, apricot, pink, and red on well-branched plants. Among them, 'Venus' has coral-pink blooms, 'Apollo' dark red, and 'Mei-Kyo', magenta. Hammer or split woody stems, dip ends in two to three inches of hot water, and stand in deep water for a few hours. Before arranging remove only foliage that falls below the waterline; foliage of mums helps to prolong their longevity. Flowers will last up to two weeks; three with a preservative added to the vase water. Many mums shatter quickly when dried. Experiment by placing flowers face up in silica gel in the microwave.

Echinops ritro, globe thistle; to 4', z3. Sun; ordinary garden soil. Quantities of bristly blue globes of flowers about two inches in diameter bloom in summer into fall. To assure long vase life as cut flowers, prevent pollination by insects by covering flower heads with mesh fabric. Cut when about half the sphere has turned blue, and condition in warm or cold water overnight. To dry, pick heads before they bloom to prevent shattering afterward; stand stems upright in a container to take on interesting curves while drying, or hang upside down. Coarse textured leaves turn silver and are effective in dried arrangements.

Gaillardia × grandiflora hybrids, gaillardia, blanket flower; to 3', z3. Sun; well-drained lean soil. Summer-blooming showy daisylike flowers to three inches across in bright yellow, orange, and red, often bicolored petals. 'Burgundy' is dark red, and plants of the Monarch strain are free-blooming over many weeks until fall. Pick as for all daisies, when blooms are fully opened but centers still tight. Remove lower leaves and split stems. Add sugar to conditioning water, about one tablespoon to a quart, and let stand overnight. Hang upside-down to air-dry.

Hemerocallis, daylily. Hybrids to 4', z3. Sun; will grow in many different kinds of soil. Over a thousand cultivars appear each year in various colors and color combinations, flower forms, heights, and bloom times. Select flowers seen in bloom to assure getting the desired colors. 'Stella d'Oro' is canary yellow and reblooms through fall. 'Ruffled Apricot' has fragrant blooms that open in the evening. 'Catherine Woodbury' is pale orchid-pink with a green throat. Select stems for cutting when at least one flower is open and buds are showing color; others will continue to open in water. Individual flowers last but a day and wither or close at night. Use in informal bouquets in which removing faded blossoms will not spoil the intended effect, or float several flowers in a shallow bowl. Individual flowers will last a day without water and may be placed directly on a table as a centerpiece or at each place setting. To assure that buds of day-blooming varieties stay open for an evening party, refrigerate sprays during the day. A stem will last a week or more in water. Thick-petaled varieties may be dried in silica gel.

Heuchera × brizoides hybrids, alumroot; to 2½', z3. Sun, part shade; damp but well-drained humusy soil. Airy sprays of tiny bell-shaped flowers on wiry stems over mats of rounded ivy-shaped leaves in June. 'Chatterbox' is a good pink, 'Queen of Hearts' is salmon, and 'Snowflake' has white flowers. Foliage is often outstanding, sometimes marbled or mottled. Cut when about half the flowers in a spray are open; buds of larger-flowered hybrids will open. Condition in warm water for a few hours. Foliage is also good for cutting; submerge leaves for a few hours in cold water. Leaves may also be preserved in glycerin. Bury flower sprays in silica gel for dried arrangements.

H. micrantha 'Palace Purple', excellent foliage, scalloped metallic coppery purple. Sprays of tiny white flowers, tinged with purple. Cut and condition as above.

Hosta, hosta, plantain lily, funkia; many species and varieties in varying heights, z3. Part shade to light shade for best flowering, but will tolerate full sun if soil is kept moist; rich, moist soil is ideal. Good foliage plant with ribbed, smooth, or puckered leaves in many shades of green and variegations with white, yellow, or cream. Varying bloom times from June until fall. Flowers in white to lavender, often fragrant, some large and showy. Cut flowers when a few blooms have opened and condition in room-temperature water. If leaves are picked early in the season, before June, dip the stem ends in a few inches of hot

water and then submerge them in cold water for several hours until crisp. May be stored in refrigerator. Condition mature leaves same as flowers. Pick seed heads before they have opened and stand in a few inches of water until coal-black seed clusters are revealed; these make unusual ornaments for winter displays. Press individual leaves between sheets of newspaper under a heavy weight for dried arrangements. (Follow these guidelines for conditioning all hosta species.)

H. decorate 'Thomas Hogg' has dark green leaves with white edging, deep-lilac bell-shaped blooms in summer on two-foot scapes.

H. plantaginea 'Grandiflora' has smooth foliage and showy double fragrant flowers in August on strong scapes to two feet.

H. ventricosa 'Piedmont Gold' has heart-shaped golden leaves and scapes of white flowers in midsummer.

Liatris aspera, blazing star, gayfeather; to 5', z3. Sun; fertile soil but tolerates heat and drought. The most elegant of the genus. Stiff bottle-brushes of small flower heads well spaced along the ends of unbranched, leafy, wandlike stems. Blooms open almost simultaneously, or from the top of the spike down. 'September Glory' has mauve-purple flowers, 'Alba' is a white variety. Cut when flowers begin to open and buds are fat. Split woody stems of older plants and condition in cold water. To dry, gather stems when most of the flowers have opened and hang upside down.

Lysimachia clethroides, gooseneck loosestrife; to 3', z3. Sun or part shade, moist soil. Slender spiky racemes of tiny white starry flowers bloom from July to September. Tips of the racemes arch downward into graceful S-curves. Cut when half the flowers on a stem are open.

Regular conditioning in water for several hours. Will last several days, or a week or more with floral preservative or a tablespoon of sugar added to vase water. Dry in silica gel for two or three days, or about ten hours in silica gel in a warm oven.

Lythrum salicaria hybrids, purple loosestrife, European loosestrife; to 6', z3. Sun or part shade; moist soil. Check with the county extension service in your area for guidance on whether loosestrife is a local nuisance because of its invasiveness; the plant is outlawed in several states. Slender flower spikes on wiry stems bloom all summer into fall. Plant only modern garden cultivars, which are not as aggressive as the species, and keep them in the border or cutting garden where they can be controlled. 'Morden's Pink', 'Dropmore Purple', and 'The Beacon', a rose red, each provide good vertical effects in bouquets. Cut flower spikes when half open and place in warm to hot water (80° to 100° F.) to start, allowing water to cool overnight. To dry, hang upside down.

Narcissus, daffodil; to 1½', z3. Sun; deep rich friable soil is ideal, but will grow in a wide range of soils with good drainage. Remarkable range of size, form, and color, from extra early to extra late bloom times. Short trumpet varieties good for arranging are 'Ice Follies', which is ivory with a chartreuse trumpet lightening to cream, and 'Barrett Browning', which is white with a large flat orange crown. Classic trumpet daffodils are 'King Alfred', which is yellow, and 'Mount Hood', which opens creamy yellow and turns white. 'Peaches and Cream' and 'Salome' have pink and apricot crowns respectively. 'Trevithian' has two to four small lemon-yellow flowers on each stem, 'Manley' carries huge double yellow flowers that resemble camellias. Cut daffodils with long stems when they are half open. Cut off white pulp at base of stems, make a vertical slit a few inches up the stem and hold cut ends under warm water for about a minute to check the flow of sticky sap. Condition separately from other cut flowers in deep water for several hours to avoid sap clogging stems of other flowers. Daffodils are most effective arranged by themselves or with flowering branches. Open flowers will last several days.

Platycodon grandiflorus, balloon flower; to 2½', z3. Sun, part shade in the South; well-drained loamy soil. In summer inflated flower buds on erect stems open to solitary, two-inch bell-shaped flowers similar to those of campanulas. Besides basic blues, some of which are double flowered ('Double Blue'), varieties come in pink ('Shell Pink') and white ('Albus' and 'Snowflake'). Cut when at least two flowers on a stem are open; the fat balloons will open later in water, tight buds will not. Sear stem ends and condition overnight in warm water. Will last from a week to ten days in an arrangement. Dry blossoms in sand.

Primula japonica, Japanese primrose; to 2½', z4. Light shade; moist soil, high in organic matter. Rugged, reliable plants with sturdy stems bearing as many as five whorled tiers of one-inch flowers in May and early June. 'Millar's Crimson', 'Etna', and 'Postford White' are good cultivars for cutting. Hybrids in offbeat orange-red, yellow, and copper shades are also available. Cut when the lower two tiers of flowers have opened and remaining buds are plump. Condition overnight in deep warm water. Recutting stems in a few days will extend vase life. Will last about a week. Not recommended for drying.

Rudbeckia fulgida, rudbeckia, orange coneflower; 2', z3. Full sun to part shade; ordinary garden soil. Orange-yellow daisylike flowers, darker orange near the central brownish disks. Flowers bloom continuously on upright branching stems from late July to mid-September. Some are bicolored with dark velvety centers. *R. f.* var. *sullivantii* 'Goldsturm' is orange-yellow with four-inch flower heads. Pick when petals unfold but while centers are still tight. Split ends and condition overnight in cool water with foliage left on. Remove lower foliage before arranging. Flowers will last a week to ten days. Flowers dry well in silica gel. Central disks are ornamental after petals drop and can be air-dried for winter bouquets.

Salvia × *superba,* hybrid sage; to 2', z5. Sun; well-drained soil. Many slender spikes of dark violet flowers from half an inch to an inch across with reddish bracts. Aromatic gray-green foliage on branching upright stems. 'May Night' has velvety dark-indigo flowers and purple bracts on foot-long stems. 'Blue Queen' has deep-violet flowers. Both bloom in May and June; if kept cut will bloom all summer. Cut when half the flowers on a spike are open. Dip stem ends briefly in a few inches of boiling water and let stand in warm water for several hours. Hang mature flower spikes upside down to air-dry.

Tanacetum parthenium, feverfew; to 3', z4. Sun, part shade; will grow in a wide range of soils. A biennial or short-lived perennial that self-sows prolifically, offering blooms all summer into fall. Profuse clusters of buttonlike white daisylike flowers with yellow disks and bright green aromatic ferny leaves. 'Ultra Double White' has fully double blooms. Cut when about half the flowers in a spray are open. Split woody stems and condition for a few hours in warm water before arranging. Will last a week. To dry, remove foliage and hang upside down.

Tulipa, tulip; to 3', z3. Prefer sun, but will bloom in part shade; loamy, well-drained soil. Numerous varieties and hybrids in myriad colors for a succession of bloom from March through May. 'Red Emperor', an early Fosteriana, is fiery red. 'Bellona' is clear yellow, fragrant, and blooms in mid-April. 'Apricot Beauty' is a fragrant, salmon-apricot triumph tulip and blooms in early May, good for forcing. 'Angelique' is a blended pink, peony-flowering tulip, and blooms in early May. 'White Parrot' has large flowers, white with touches of green on petals, flowering in May. 'Queen of Sheba' is a lily-flowering tulip with reflexed petals in red, flowering in May. 'Queen of the Night' is a deep velvety maroon cottage tulip and blooms in late May. Cut as buds begin to open. Trim off white pulp at base of stems. To keep stems straight and flowers from drooping while conditioning, wrap stems in bunches in wet newspaper reaching up to flower buds and stand in cold water overnight. Best arranged by themselves or with spring branches, as flowers will open and close and turn toward light, and stems will continue to grow. Frequent recutting extends vase life. Will last several days to a week.

Veronica longifolia, veronica, speedwell; to 4', z4. Full sun for best flowering, but will tolerate part shade; ordinary well-drained soil, although it will tolerate drought. 'Sunny Border Blue', a hybrid, bears dark violet-blue flowers on dense spikes throughout the summer into September. Cut when flower spikes are half open and condition in warm water. Will last several days to a week. Air-dry flower spikes, or dry in sand or silica gel.

Herbs for Bouquets

Unless indicated otherwise, most herbs grow best in full sun and well-drained soil, preferably sandy loam. Many will tolerate part shade, but aromatic herbs need full sun to develop their essential oils.

Allium spp., ornamental onion. Perennial. Flowers, seed heads.

Anethum graveolens, dill. Annual. Flowers in yellow umbels, ferny aromatic foliage.

Artemisia spp. Annual, perennial. Aromatic gray foliage, tiny flower clusters.

Foeniculum vulgare, fennel. Perennial grown as an annual. Sulfur, lacy flower heads. Also, bronze form. Ferny anise-scented foliage. Attractive seed heads.

Lavandula angustifolia and cultivars, English lavender. Perennial. Prefers alkaline soil. Scented lavender flower spikes, gray foliage.

Melissa officinalis, lemon balm. Perennial. Foliage.

Mentha spp., mint. Perennial. Most species grow rampantly, especially in part shade and moist soil. Ginger-, pineapple-, peppermint-scented foliage, etc.; lavender or white flower spikes.

Myrrhis odorata, sweet cicely. Perennial. Needs humusy soil. White lacy flowers. Seed heads.

Ocimum basilicum 'Crispum', lettuce leaf basil. Annual. White flowers. Good smooth leaves, puffed in center, makes attractive greenery in bouquets.

O. b. purpurascens, purple basil. Annual. 'Dark Opal' has pink flowers, purple "lettuce" leaves, effective with annuals in bouquets.

Origanum majorana, sweet marjoram. Perennial grown as an annual. Foliage.

O. vulgare and cultivars, oregano. Perennial. Small pink flowers, reddish bracts; or white with green bracts. Useful foliage, variegated form also.

Pelargonium spp., scented geraniums. Perennial. Delicate flowers; apple-, lemon-, pineapple-, rose-, cinnamon-scented, etc., leaves.

Perilla frutescens, perilla. Annual. Metallic burgundy foliage; spiky seed heads.

Petroselinum crispum, parsley. Biennial. Ferny foliage.

Rosmarinus officinalis and cultivars, rosemary. Perennial. Piny, resinous needle-like foliage, tiny blue flowers.

Ruta graveolens, rue. Perennial. Steel-blue foliage, yellow flowers, and seed heads good in dried arrangements.

Salvia officinalis, sage. Perennial. Gray, rough-textured foliage. 'Purpurascens' has purplish leaves.

Symphytum spp., comfrey. Perennial. Tolerates shade; thrives in moist soil. Showy pink flower buds opening to nodding blue flowers. (Large architectural plant; invasive if not kept in check.)

Valeriana officinalis, garden heliotrope. Perennial. Tolerates shade. Fragrant flowers.

Ornamental Perennial Grasses

Unless indicated otherwise, grasses flower best in a sunny location and will adapt to a wide range of soil conditions.

Briza media, quaking grass; to 3', z4. Similar to *B. maxima* and *B. minor*, which are annuals, this hardy, loose, and airy perennial, about 18 inches high, puts out two- to three-foot flower stalks carrying trembling fat spikelets in spring. Green at first, fading to beige, with heart-shaped seed heads. Excellent cut either fresh or for drying.

Calamagrostis × *acutiflora*, feather reed grass; to 6', z5. 'Karl Foerster', an early season bloomer, begins to send up two- to three-foot-long feathery spires of flowers in June. Flowers turn from pink to dark purplish pink and finally a golden tan color in fall. A good choice for gardens with a short growing season.

C. × *acutiflora stricta* is slightly taller than 'Karl Foerster', to 7', z5. Blooms about two weeks later with reddish bronze inflorescences that become tawny in autumn. Flowers and foliage hold up well into winter.

Deschampsia caespitosa, tufted hair grass; to 2', z4. Will take part shade, prefers moist soil. Several similar cultivars feature loose, delicate inflorescences on slender stalks and come in various shades of golden and light yellow. Blooms from summer until fall. 'Dew Carrier' is a heavy bloomer with flower spikes a yard high.

Erianthus ravennae, ravenna grass; to over 12', z6. Will take part shade; prefers moist soil. A vase-shaped clump of silvery foliage, called the "pampas grass" of the North. Silvery purple, silky, dense flower panicles, two feet long, shoot up above the foliage in late summer.

E. strictus is a smaller species of Ravenna grass, to 6', z6. Will grow well in wet soils as well as in humusy garden soil and in part shade. Good flowers and autumn color.

Miscanthus sinensis, Japanese silver grass; cultivars to 9', z5. Over two dozen cultivars offer a range of heights, subtle flower colors, and elegance of its bladed foliage. 'Graziella' has slender foliage and two-foot white fan-shaped plumes on six-foot-long strong stalks in August. Foliage becomes golden bronze in early winter.

M. s. 'Gracillimus', maiden grass; to 8', z5. Vase-shaped, finely narrow foliage and silken, bronze-red panicles turning to silver on eight-foot stalks. Blooms in early October. Autumnal tawny sheaves and dried seed heads hold into winter.

M. s. 'Variegatus', variegated Japanese silver grass; to 7', z6. Variegated foliage with cream-colored vertical stripes. Blooms in late September. 'Morning Light' has silver variegated leaves and silvery white flowers; October blooming.

M. s. zebrinus, zebra grass; to 8', z6. Will take part shade; prefers moist humusy soil. Unique yellow or creamy white horizontal bands distinguishes this grass from the other forms of miscanthus. A nice specimen plant, very effective planted on the edges of a pond or water garden. Feather-duster flower plumes in silvery white, four feet above the foliage. Foliage imparts an exotic touch to arrangements. Long-stemmed plumes may be dried and arranged in a tall container such as an umbrella stand and placed on the floor.

Molinia caerulea, purple moor grass; to 3', z5. Will tolerate part shade; thrives in slightly acidic moist soils. Graceful leaf blades taper to a fine point in neat clumps. In June dense clouds of airy purplish inflorescences, about eight inches long, are borne on five-foot stems. 'Variegata' has leaf blades striped green and cream, and is especially attractive in fresh arrangements.

Panicum virgatum, switch grass; loose clumps to 8', z5. Foliage is often curly at ends, offering swirled lines for arrangements; it may also be metallic blue, as in 'Heavy Metal', to five feet; or red, becoming more intense in autumn, as in 'Squaw' and 'Warrior', to four feet. Pink clouds of flower heads in late July and August are good for cutting; seed heads dry to a wheat color.

P. v. 'Haense Herms', red switch grass; to 4', z5. Pink inflorescences rise two feet above the foliage in late summer. Foliage is effective for many months, beginning as blue-green blades to two feet, and turning intense red in autumn.

Pennisetum alopecuroides, fountain grass; to 4', z6. Narrow arching foliage in various shades of green and burgundy. In August, bristly flower spikelets appear in pinkish mauve or crimson bottle-brush flower heads almost a foot long. 'Hameln' and the similar 'Weserbergland' grow to only two or three feet and are fine choices for the front or middle of a mixed border.

SOURCES

The cross section of garden suppliers listed here is but a sampling of the many companies, large and small, that carry seeds, plants, tools, garden equipment and supplies, and books; many also stand by to offer advice and other services. Each company's specialty is indicated, but most also handle a broader range of plants. Many companies charge a small fee (usually refundable with a purchase) for a catalog; it is a good idea to enclose a self-addressed stamped envelope when writing for information. The list can be expanded by consulting specialized books devoted to this subject, such as *Gardening by Mail* and *Taylor's Guide to Specialty Nurseries*, by Barbara J. Barton (Houghton Mifflin), and *The Gardener's Book of Sources*, compiled by William Bryant Logan (Penguin Books, 1988).

General: Ornamental and Edible Seeds and Plants; Garden Supplies

W. Atlee Burpee & Co.
300 Park Avenue
Warminster, PA 18974
Wide range of edible and ornamental seeds and plants, tools and garden supplies.

Carroll Gardens
444 E. Main Street
P.O. Box 310
Westminster, MD 21157
Plants of perennials, grasses, herbs, shrubs, trees, roses, bulbs.

Gurney's Seed & Nursery Co.
110 Capital Street
Yankton, SD 57079
Seeds, bulbs, plants, trees and shrubs.

Harris Seeds
60 Saginaw Drive
P.O. Box 22960
Rochester, NY 14692-2960
Good selection of perennials, and much more.

Johnny's Selected Seeds
Foss Hill Road
Albion, ME 04910-9731
Short-season flower, herb, and vegetable seeds; garden supplies.

Mellinger's
2310 W. South Range Road
North Lima, OH 44452-9731
Very wide range of edible and ornamental seeds and plants, including ornamental trees and shrubs; many garden supplies.

Park Seed Co.
Cokesbury Road
Greenwood, SC 29647-0001
Seeds, plants, bulbs, annuals, perennials, shrubs.

Stokes Seeds Inc.
P.O. Box 548
Buffalo, NY 14240
Flower and vegetable seeds.

Thompson & Morgan Inc.
P.O. Box 1308
Jackson, NJ 08527-0308
Wide range of seeds, and a few plants, for flowers, ornamental grasses, and some vegetables.

Wayside Gardens
1 Garden Lane
Hodges, SC 29695-0001
Wide selection of flowering trees, shrubs, perennials, bulbs, and grasses; selected roses, including David Austin hybrids.

White Flower Farm
Litchfield, CT 06759-0050
Perennials, selected shrubs, bulbs.

Specialty Plants and Bulbs

Blackmore & Langdon
Pensford
Bristol, BS18 4JL
England
Seeds of delphiniums and polyanthus primroses.

Kurt Bluemel, Inc.
2740 Greene Lane
Baldwin, MD 21013-9523
Ornamental grasses, bamboo, and perennials.

Blue Dahlia Gardens
P.O. Box 316
San Jose, IL 62682
Dahlias.

Busse Gardens
Route 2, Box 238
Cokato, MN 55321-9426
Perennials, including hostas, daylilies, astilbe, phlox, species irises, herbaceous and tree peonies.

Cooper's Garden
212 W. County Road C
Roseville, MN 55113
Species, tall-bearded, Siberian irises.

Klehm Nursery
Route 5, Box 197
Penny Road
South Barrington, IL 60010-9555
Herbaceous and tree peonies, hostas, daylilies, astilbes.

Oakes Daylilies
8204 Monday Road
Corryton, TN 37721
Daylilies

Pleasant Valley Glads
P.O. Box 494
Agawam, MA 01001
Tall and miniature gladioluses.

Rocknoll Nursery
1639 Hess Road
Sardinia, OH 45191
Perennials.

The Thomas Jefferson Center for
Historic Plants
Monticello, P.O. Box 318
Charlottesville, VA 22902
*Seeds harvested from gardens of Monticello and
other seeds of historic varieties.*

Tranquil Lake Nursery
45 River Street
Rehoboth, MA 02769-1395
Japanese and Siberian irises, daylilies.

Van Bourgondien Brothers
P.O. Box 1000
245 Farmingdale Road
Baylon, NY 11702
*Peonies, dahlias, lilies, gladioluses, and other
perennials.*

André Viette Farm & Nursery
Route 1, Box 16
Fishersville, VA 22939
Perennials, large selection of daylilies.

Herbs

Gilbertie's Herb Gardens
7 Sylvan Lane
Westport, CT 06880
No mail orders; open year round.

Merry Gardens
P.O. Box 595
Mechanic Street
Camden, ME 04843

Nichols Garden Nursery
1190 North Pacific Highway
Albany, OR 97321-4598

Richters
Goodwood, ON LOC 1A0
Canada

Roses

High Country Rosarium
1717 Downing Street
Denver, CO 80218
Old, species, and shrub roses.

Jackson & Perkins
1 Rose Lane
Medford, OR 97501
Modern roses and bulbs.

Pickering Nurseries, Inc.
670 Kingston Road
Highway 2
Pickering, ON L1V 1A6
Canada
*Wide selection of old and hard-to-find roses;
modern roses; David Austin hybrids.*

Roses of Yesterday and Today
802 Brown's Valley Road
Watsonville, CA 95076-0398
Old and selected modern roses.

Flowering Bulbs

B & D Lilies
330 "P" Street
Port Townsend, WA 98368

The Daffodil Mart
Route 3, Box 794
Gloucester, VA 23061

McClure & Zimmerman
108 W. Winnebago Street
P.O. Box 368
Friesland, WI 53935

Rex Bulb Farms
P.O. Box 774
4310-B Highway 20
Port Townsend, WA 98368
Hybrid and species lilies.

John Scheepers, Inc.
P.O. Box 700
Bantam, CT 06750

Azaleas and Rhododendrons

Cardinal Nursery
Route 1, Box 316
State Road, NC 28676

Carlson's Gardens
P.O. Box 305
South Salem, NY 10590

Kelleygreen Rhododendron Nursery
P.O. Box 42
6924 Highway 38
Drain, OR 97435

Roslyn Nursery
211 Burrs Lane
Dix Hills, NY 11746

Westgate Garden Nursery
751 Westgate Drive
Eureka, CA 95503

Trees and Shrubs

Camellia Forest Nursery
125 Carolina Forest Road
Chapel Hill, NC 27516

Girard Nurseries
P.O. Box 428
Geneva, OH 44041

Greer Gardens
1280 Goodpasture Island Road
Eugene, OR 97401

Heronswood Nursery
7530 288th Street NE
Kingston, WA 98346
Choice trees, shrubs, perennials, and grasses.

Lake County Nursery Inc.
P.O. Box 122
Perry, OH 44081
Wholesaler; order through your garden center.

Miller Nurseries
5060 West Lake Road
Canandaigua, NY 14424

Valley Nursery
P.O. Box 4845
2801 N. Montana Ave.
Helena, MT 59604

Weston Nurseries
P.O. Box 186
E. Main Street
Hopkinton, MA 01748
Wholesale and retail only.

Wildflowers and Native Plants

Applewood Seed Co.
5380 Vivian Street
Arvada, CO 80002

Gardens of the Blue Ridge
P.O. Box 10
Pineola, NC 28662

Little Valley Farm
RR3, Box 544
Spring Green, WI 53588

Native Gardens
5737 Fisher Lane
Greenback, TN 37742

Clyde Robin Seed Company
P.O. Box 2366
Castro Valley, CA 94546

Vermont Wildflower Farm
Route 7, P.O. Box 5
Charlotte, VT 05445

Tools and Equipment

Gardener's Eden
P.O. Box 7307
San Francisco, CA 94120-7307

Gardener's Supply Co.
128 Intervale Road
Burlington, VT 05401

A. M. Leonard, Inc.
P.O. Box 816
Piqua, OH 45356-0816

Smith & Hawken
25 Corte Madera
Mill Valley, CA 94941

BIBLIOGRAPHY AND
SUGGESTED READING

A good garden book can afford almost as much pleasure as gardening itself. Literally thousands of books are available, covering every aspect of landscape and garden history, design, and techniques. They range from no-nonsense reference and how-to books to those delightful books that share personal experiences and philosophies, sometimes written by opinionated, often idiosyncratic, individuals who have conducted a passionate love affair with gardening over the better part of a lifetime. Some of these books are classics, and others have been written by contemporaries. Several are now out of print but can be borrowed from libraries or found through specialty booksellers. The following is a personal selection of those that I hope you will find helpful and inspiring.

Sources that were consulted in preparing this book are marked with an asterisk. Most useful were *Perennials for American Gardens*, by Ruth Rogers Clausen and Nicolas H. Ekstrom; *Gardening for Flower Arrangement*, by Arno Nehrling and Irene Nehrling; and *The Decorative Art of Dried Flower Arrangement*, by Georgia S. Vance. *Manual of Woody Landscape Plants*, by Michael A. Dirr, provided the major source of information on shrubs and trees, and is used with the author's permission.

Landscape and Garden Design

Appleton, Bonnie Lee. *Landscape Rejuvenation*. Pownal, Vermont: Storey Communications, 1991.

*Brookes, John. *The Book of Garden Design*. New York: Macmillan, 1991.

———. *The Small Garden Book*. Avenah, New Jersey: Outlet Book Co., 1991.

*Church, Thomas D., Grace Hall, and Michael Laurie. *Gardens Are for People*. 2nd revised edition. New York: McGraw-Hill, 1983.

Crowe, Sylvia. *Garden Design*. London: Packard Publishing, 1981.

Douglas, William L., and others. *Garden Design*. New York: Simon and Schuster, 1984.

Downing, Andrew Jackson. *A Treatise on the Theory and Practice of Landscape Gardening Adapted to North America*. Little Compton, Rhode Island: Theophrastus Press, 1976. Originally published in 1856 by D. Appleton and Co., New York.

Frederick, William H., Jr. *The Exuberant Garden and the Controlling Hand*. Boston: Little, Brown, 1992.

Glattstein, Judy. *Garden Design with Foliage*. Pownal, Vermont: Storey Communications, 1991.

*Harper, Pamela J. *Designing with Perennials*. New York: Macmillan, 1991.

*Hobhouse, Penelope. *Color in Your Garden*. Boston: Little, Brown, 1985.

———. *Flower Gardens*. Boston: Little, Brown, 1992.

———. *Borders*. New York: Harper and Row, 1989.

Ireys, Alice Recknagel. *Design for American Gardens*. New York: Prentice-Hall, 1991.

*Jekyll, Gertrude. *Colour Schemes for the Flower Garden*. Salem, New Hampshire: Ayer, 1983. Originally published as *Colour in the Flower Garden* in 1908 by Country Life, London.

*———. *Wood and Garden*. Salem, New Hampshire: Ayer, 1983.

Originally published in 1899 by Longmans, Green, London.

Keen, Mary. *The Garden Border Book*. Deer Park, Wisconsin: Capability's Books, 1987.

Lees, Carlton B. *New Budget Landscaping*. New York: Holt, Rinehart and Winston, 1979.

Lovejoy, Ann. *The American Mixed Border*. New York: Macmillan, 1993.

Reader's Digest Practical Guide to Home Landscaping. Pleasantville, New York: Reader's Digest, 1977.

*Robinson, Florence Bell. *Planting Design*. New York: McGraw-Hill, 1940.

Smith, Mary Riley. *The Front Garden*. Boston: Houghton Mifflin, 1991.

*Smyser, Carol A., and editors of Rodale Press. *Nature's Design*. Emmaus, Pennsylvania: Rodale Press, 1992.

Verey, Rosemary. *Classic Garden Design*. New York: Random House, 1989.

*———. *The Flower Arranger's Garden*. Boston: Little, Brown, 1989.

*Wilder, Louise Beebe. *Color in My Garden*. New York: Atlantic Monthly Press, 1990. Originally published in 1918 by Doubleday, Garden City, New York.

Reference and Gardening Technique

*Armitage, Allan. *Herbaceous Perennial Plants*. Athens, Georgia: Varsity Press, 1989.

Baumgardt, John Philip. *How to Prune Almost Everything*. New York: M. Barrows, 1968.

Beales, Peter. *Roses: An Illustrated Encyclopedia and Grower's Handbook of Species Roses, Old and Modern Roses, Shrub Roses and Climbers.* New York: Henry Holt, 1992.

Bryan, John. *Bulbs.* 2 volumes. Portland, Oregon: Timber Press, 1989.

Bush-Brown, James and Louise. *America's Garden Book.* Revised edition. New York: Charles Scribner's Sons, 1980.

Christopher, Thomas. *In Search of Lost Roses.* New York: Summit Books, 1989.

*Crockett, James Underwood, and the editors of Time-Life Books, eds. *Time-Life Encyclopedia of Gardening: Trees, Evergreens, Flowering Shrubs, Annuals, Perennials.* New York: Time-Life Books, 1971–1972.

*Cruso, Thalassa. *Making Things Grow Outdoors.* New York: Alfred A. Knopf, 1974.

*Dirr, Michael A. *Manual of Woody Landscape Plants.* 4th edition. Champaign, Illinois: Stipes, 1990.

Eddison, Sydney. *A Passion for Daylilies.* New York: HarperCollins, 1992.

Greenlee, John. *The Encyclopedia of Ornamental Grasses.* Emmaus, Pennsylvania: Rodale Press, 1992.

Grieve, Maud. *A Modern Herbal.* New York: Dover, 1971. Originally published in 1931 by Harcourt, Brace, New York.

Harper, Pamela, and Frederick McGourty. *Perennials.* Los Angeles: HP Books, 1982.

*Hériteau, Jacqueline, with Dr. H. Marc Cathey and the staff and consultants of the U.S. National Arboretum. *The National Arboretum Book of Outstanding Garden Plants.* New York: Simon and Schuster, 1990.

Hightshoe, Gary L. *Native Trees, Shrubs and Vines for Urban and Rural America.* New York: Van Nostrand Reinhold, 1987.

Hill, Lewis. *Pruning Simplified.* Updated edition. Pownal, Vermont: Storey Communications, 1986.

Huxley, Anthony, and Mark Griffiths, eds. *The New Royal Horticultural Society Dictionary of Gardening.* 4 volumes. New York: Stockton Press, 1992.

Johnson, Hugh. *The Principles of Gardening.* New York: Simon and Schuster, 1982.

Lacy, Allen. *The Garden in Autumn.* New York: Atlantic Monthly Press, 1990.

Lloyd, Christopher. *Foliage Plants.* Revised edition. New York: Random House, 1973.

*———. *The Well-Tempered Garden.* Revised edition. New York: Random House, 1985.

———, and Tom Bennett. *Clematis.* Revised edition. Deer Park, Wisconsin: Capability's Books, 1989.

*Loewer, Peter. *Growing and Decorating with Grasses.* New York: Walker and Co., 1977.

McGourty, Frederick. *The Perennial Gardener.* Boston: Houghton Mifflin, 1989.

Oakes, A. J. *Ornamental Grasses and Grasslike Plants.* New York: Van Nostrand Reinhold, 1990.

*Ottesen, Carole. *Ornamental Grasses: The Amber Wave.* New York: McGraw-Hill, 1989.

Phillips, Roger, and Martyn Rix. *Shrubs.* New York: Random House, 1989.

*Proctor, Rob. *Antique Flowers: Annuals.* New York: HarperCollins, 1991.

*———. *Antique Flowers: Perennials.* New York: Harper and Row, 1990.

*Robinson, William. *The English Flower Garden.* New York: Amaryllis Press, 1984. Reprint of the 15th edition, originally published in 1933 by J. Murray, London.

Rodale's All-New Encyclopedia of Organic Gardening: The Indispensable Resource for Every Gardener. Bradley, Fern Marshall, and Barbara W. Ellis, eds. Emmaus, Pennsylvania: Rodale Press, 1992.

Salley, Homer E., and Harold E. Greer. *Rhododendron Hybrids.* Portland, Oregon: Timber Press, 1986.

Scanniello, Stephen, and Tania Bayard. *Roses of America: The Brooklyn Botanic Garden's Guide to Our National Flower.* New York: Henry Holt, 1990.

Sedgwick, Mabel C. *The Garden Month by Month.* New York: Frederick A. Stokes, 1907.

*Staff of the Liberty Hyde Bailey Hortorium, Cornell University. *Hortus Third.* New York: Macmillan, 1976.

Steffek, Edwin F. *The Pruning Manual.* 2nd revised edition. New York: Van Nostrand Reinhold, 1982.

Taylor's Guides to Gardening: *Annuals; Perennials; Bulbs; Ground Covers, Vines & Grasses; Trees; Shrubs; Roses.* Boston: Houghton Mifflin, 1986–1987.

*Thomas, Graham Stuart. *Perennial Garden Plants.* Revised edition. London: J. M. Dent and Sons, 1982.

*———. *Ornamental Shrubs, Climbers and Bamboos.* Portland, Oregon: Sagapress/Timber Press, 1992.

———. *The Old Shrub Roses.* London: J. M. Dent and Sons, 1980.

Westcott, Cynthia. *The Gardener's Bug Book.* 4th edition. Garden City, New York: Doubleday, 1973.

Winterrowd, Wayne. *Annuals for Connoisseurs.* New York: Prentice-Hall, 1992.

Wright, Michael. *The Complete Handbook of Garden Plants.* New York: Facts on File, 1984.

Wyman, Donald. *Trees for American Gardens.* 3rd edition. New York: Macmillan, 1990.

*Zucker, Isabel. *Flowering Shrubs and Small Trees.* Revised edition. New York: Grove Press, 1990.

Regional and Specialized Gardening

*Druse, Ken. *The Natural Garden.* New York: Clarkson N. Potter, 1988.

———. *The Natural Shade Garden.* New York: Clarkson N. Potter, 1992.

Hunt, William L. *Southern Gardening.* Durham, North Carolina: Duke University Press, 1982.

Lawrence, Elizabeth. *A Southern Garden: A Handbook for the Middle South.* Revised edition. Chapel Hill: University of North Carolina Press, 1984. Originally published in 1941.

Lovejoy, Ann. *The Year in Bloom: A Northwest Garden through the Seasons.* Seattle: Sasquatch Books, 1987.

———. *The Border in Bloom: Gardening for All Seasons in the Pacific Northwest.* Seattle: Sasquatch Books, 1990.

McDonald, Elvin. *Northeast Gardening: The Diverse Art and Special Considerations of Gardening in the Northeast.* New York: Macmillan, 1990.

*Nehrling, Arno, and Irene Nehrling. *Gardening for Flower Arrangement.* New York: Dover, 1976. Originally published in 1969 as *Flower Growing for Flower Arrangement* by Hearthside Press, Great Neck, New York.

Oehme, Wolfgang, and James van Sweden. *Bold Romantic Gardens.* Herndon, Virginia: Acropolis Books, 1990.

*Ottesen, Carole. *The New American Garden.* New York: Macmillan, 1987.

Schenk, George. *The Complete Shade Garden.* Boston: Houghton Mifflin, 1984.

Snyder, Rachel. *Gardening in the Heartland.* Lawrence: University Press of Kansas, 1992.

Sperry, Neil. *Complete Guide to Texas Gardening.* Dallas, Texas: Taylor Publishing, 1982.

Sunset Magazine and Book Editors. *Sunset Western Garden Book.* 4th edition. Menlo Park, California: Sunset, 1988.

Taylor's Regional Guides to Gardening Series. *The South; The Southwest and Southern California.* Boston: Houghton Mifflin, 1992.

Wilson, James W. *Landscaping with Wildflowers: An Environmental Approach to Gardening.* Boston: Houghton Mifflin, 1992.

Yang, Linda. *The City Gardener's Handbook.* New York: Random House, 1990.

Garden History and General

Clifford, Derek. *A History of Garden Design.* New York: Frederick A. Praeger, 1986.

Dickey, Page. *Duck Hill Journal.* Boston: Houghton Mifflin, 1991.

*Ely, Helena Rutherfurd. *A Woman's Hardy Garden.* New York: Macmillan, 1990. Originally published in 1903 by Macmillan.

Griswold, Mack, and Eleanor Weller. *The Golden Age of American Gardens.* New York: Abrams, 1991.

Harvey, John. *Mediaeval Gardens.* London: B. T. Batsford, 1981.

Jefferson, Thomas. *Thomas Jefferson's Garden Book (1766–1824).* Philadelphia: American Philosophical Society, 1974. Originally published in *Memoirs of the American Philosophical Society,* Volume 22 in 1944.

Leighton, Ann. *Early American Gardens.* Boston: Houghton Mifflin, 1970.

Mitchell, Henry. *The Essential Earthman.* Bloomington: Indiana University Press, 1981.

*Nichols, Beverley. *Down the Garden Path.* Garden City, New York: Doubleday, 1932.

———. *How Does Your Garden Grow?* Garden City, New York: Doubleday, 1935.

———. *Garden Open Today.* New York: Dutton, 1963.

*Page, Russell. *The Education of a Gardener.* New York: Vintage, 1985.

Perenyi, Eleanor. *Green Thoughts.* New York: Random House, 1981.

*Sackville-West, Vita. *A Joy of Gardening.* New York: Harper and Row, 1958.

Thaxter, Celia. *An Island Garden.* Boston: Houghton Mifflin, 1988.

Originally published in 1894 by Houghton Mifflin.

*White, Katharine S. *Onward and Upward in the Garden.* New York: Farrar, Straus and Giroux, 1979.

Wright, Richardson. *The Gardener's Bed-Book.* New York: PAJ Publications, 1988. Originally published in 1928 by Lippincott, New York.

*———. *Flowers for Cutting and Decoration.* New York: E. P. Dutton, 1923.

Flower Arranging with Fresh and Dried Flowers

*Burgess, Linda, with text by Susan Conder. *A Sense of the Country.* Boston: Little, Brown, 1990.

*Ferguson, J. Barry, and Tom Cowan. *Living with Flowers.* New York: Rizzoli International, 1990.

Hillier, Malcolm. *The Book of Fresh Flowers.* New York: Simon and Schuster, 1988.

———, and Colin Hilton. *The Complete Book of Dried Flowers.* New York: Simon and Schuster, 1987.

*Jekyll, Gertrude. *Flower Decoration in the House.* Woodbridge, Suffolk: Antique Collectors' Club, 1982. Originally published in 1907 by Country Life, London.

Kollath, Richard, and Carol Spier. *Year-Round Wreaths.* New York: Facts on File, 1992.

*MacQueen, Sheila. *The New Flower Arranging from Your Garden.* New York: Macmillan, 1988. Originally published in 1977 by Ward Lock, London.

*Madderlake (Tom Pritchard, Billy Jarecki, and Alan Boehmer). *Flowers Rediscovered.* New York: Stewart, Tabori and Chang, 1985.

Newdick, Jane. *Five-Minute Flower Arranger.* New York: Crown, 1989.

Ohrbach, Barbara Milo. *The Scented Room.* New York: Clarkson N. Potter, 1986.

*Otis, Denise. *Decorating with Flowers.* New York: Abrams, 1990.

*Packer, Jane. *Celebrating with Flowers.* New York: Ballantine, 1988.

Silber, Mark, and Terry Silber. *The Complete Book of Everlastings.* New York: Knopf, 1988.

Thorpe, Patricia. *Everlastings.* New York: Facts on File, 1985.

*Vance, Georgia S. *The Decorative Art of Dried Flower Arrangement.* Garden City, New York: Doubleday, 1972.

Periodicals

American Horticulturist. American Horticultural Society, 7931 East Boulevard Drive, Alexandria, Virginia 22308.

The Avant Gardener (horticultural newsletter). Horticultural Data Processors, Box 489, New York, New York 10028.

Brooklyn Botanic Garden Handbook Series. About 50 titles currently available. Brooklyn Botanic Garden, 1000 Washington Avenue, Brooklyn, New York 11225.

Fine Gardening. The Taunton Press, Box 5506, Newtown, Connecticut 06470-5506.

Flower and Garden. Flower and Garden, 4251 Pennsylvania Avenue, Kansas City, Missouri 64111-9990.

The Green Scene. The Pennsylvania Horticultural Society, 325 Walnut Street, Philadelphia, Pennsylvania 19106.

Horticulture, The Magazine of American Gardening. Horticulture Limited Partnership, 20 Park Plaza, Suite 1220, Boston, Massachusetts 02116-8241.

National Gardening. National Gardening Association, 180 Flynn Avenue, Burlington, Vermont 05401.

Rodale's Organic Gardening. Rodale Press, Inc., 33 East Minor Street, Emmaus, Pennsylvania 18093.

INDEX

ACKNOWLEDGMENTS

That gardeners are remarkably generous and delightful people was affirmed again and again as Peter Margonelli and I traveled around the country to photograph for this book. So many benign folk tidied their gardens, made bouquets, and opened their homes to us that it would be the blackest ingratitude not to mention each by name. So, at the risk of its appearing like a roster of the hundred best garden plants, I have listed their names on the facing page, along with those of my garden-writing peers, plant professionals, and friends who graciously contributed in other ways. Heartfelt thanks to one and all.

Closer to home, special thanks go to my wonderful neighbors for their long patience and unstinting support during the making of this book, especially to Henrietta Lockwood, Betsy Atkins, Dorothy Hubbell, Lucia and Dudley Bonsal, and Robin Zitter. Bouquets also go to my Saturday gardener of many years, Silvano Signora, whose good nature and innate sense of plants and four-legged intruders have been the greatest blessing. And I shall always recall with fond remembrance the late James Gibb, superb gardener, naturalist, mentor, friend.

Thanks also to my agent, Carla Glasser, for speedily finding a home for my book and for her continuing encouragement. Photographer Peter Margonelli's fine aesthetic sense combined with his skill behind a camera captured each garden and arrangement at its best to enliven these pages. Extra praise goes to Starr Lawrence, whose spirited talent was put to work in creating inspired arrangements. I am grateful to Catherine Ziegler, Dan Taylor, and Kurt Bluemel for generously taking time from their busy lives to read parts of the manuscript and to make suggestions.

I am fortunate in having as my editor, Jennie McGregor Bernard, who handled the complex editorial demands and problems of this book with admirable ability and utmost sensitivity. Her gentle prodding and pursuit of excellence constantly inspired me to renew my own efforts. My special thanks go to Sarah Longacre and her staff in the photo department for sorting through and categorizing over 1,500 slides with astonishing efficiency, and to Amanda Wilson for creatively wrapping text and photos into a visual design that embodies the spirit of the book. My thanks also to Laura Lindgren for her additional design work, Hope Koturo for handling the production, DeAnna Lunden for proofreading, and Pat Woodruff for the index. I must also acknowledge the help of Rita Buchannan in shaping the manuscript, and Betsy Strauch for expertly checking botanical names and the accuracy of endless other details.

Last, for my pussycat, Thossie, whose company and diverting antics comforted me through the long days and nights of writing this book, there can be no words to express my thanks and affection.

Nor for Bob, to whom this book is also dedicated, with my love and gratitude.

Thanks to (page numbers indicate photographs of garden or arrangement) Mr. and Mrs. Howard Adams (60 bottom, 61, 101); Betty Ajay, landscape architect (51); Allan Armitage; Betsy Atkins (11 top, 165); Linda Barksdale (34 bottom, 132 bottom, 140, 144 top left); Mr. and Mrs. George Batchelder; Bedford Free Library; Geof Beasley and Jim Sampson (3, 86, 153); Craig Bergmann and James Grigsby, landscape design (27 bottom, 89 top, 90 top, 128); Kurt Bluemel, Kurt Bluemel Inc.; Mr. and Mrs. Laurence Booth (107); Dan Borroff, landscape design (28); Sue Buckles; W. Atlee Burpee & Co., Carol Whitenack and Jonathan Burpee; Nancy Carney (40); Eleanor Carnwath; Jeanne Chappell, floral designer, dried flowers (151, 159, 160, 163); Chicago Botanical Garden, Galen Gates; Thomas Christopher; Claire's Garden Center, Janis Neubauer; Mrs. Edward Dane (147); Mrs. Linda Denison; Page Dickey (26); Ken Druse; Sydney Eddison (36–37); Mr. and Mrs. Alan Emmet (7 top, 15, 30–31, 138); Filoli, Ann Taylor and staff (33, 74 middle, 118, 134–135, 137); Laura Fisher, garden designed with Hitch Lyman (2, 21 bottom, 81, 82 left, 89 middle; arrangement by Laura Fisher, 141); Kay Flory (6 top, 24, 25, 99); Flowers by George, George von Tobel (152); Beverly Frank; Mr. and Mrs. Humes Franklin, Jr. (6 middle, 34 top, 48, 49, 75 bottom); Mrs. Thomas Fransioli; Mrs. William Goodan; Mrs. Paul Hagan and Patti Hagan; Mr. and Mrs. John Hall; Mrs. Pamela C. Harriman and her gardener and horticulturist, William Hoogeveen (9, 22–23, 66–67, 93, 110); Dr. Ellen Henke; Heronswood Nursery, Dan Hinkley and staff; Mrs. William. B. Hubbell; Mrs. Harry Hull; Mr. and Mrs. Derk Hunter (34 middle); Mr. and Mrs. Clint John (111 bottom); Mr. Evert Johnson (60 top); Nancy Johnson; Mrs. Ann Jones (16 left, 115 top); Leah Kennell, floral designer (121); Mr. and Mrs. Philip Lawrence; Starr Lawrence, floral designer (11 bottom, 14, 127, 146, 158, 165); Long Hill Reservation, Larry J. Simpson; Ann Lovejoy (39, 100 middle, 102, 103); Mr. and Mrs. Robert McBride; Nancy McCabe, landscape design (126); Cecile McCaull (24, 32, 42, 44, 70, 71, 135); Carol Mickelsen, San Benito House (8 top); Marion Miller; P. Clifford Miller Landscape Design, and Ann Miller (60 bottom, 61, 101, 107, 108, 109); Monticello, Peggy Newcomb (59); Virginia Morrell; New York Botanical Garden, thanks especially to the wonderful library staff, Lothian Lynas (now retired), Dora Galitzki, Bruce Riggs, and Gregory Piotrowski; Cynthia Nolen; Oatlands, Alfredo Siani and garden staff (88 middle, 91, 92 top); Denise Otis; Mr. and Mrs. Robert Pamplin (52); Park Seed Company, Karen Jennings; Ann and Rob Patrick, Designs in Flowers & Plantings; Mr. John W. S. Platt (95 top, right); Nancy Goslee Power; Ted and Prudence Ragsdale (111 top); Polly Reed (57, 65, 85, 98 top); Mrs. F. Turner Reuter; Renny Reynolds, floral designs and Renny The Perennial Farm (104–105, 106, 135 middle, 144–145); Mrs. Lily Rice (63); Rosedale Nurseries, Inc., Daniel L. Taylor (44 top, 45); Pauline Runkle, Floral Artistry (64 bottom, 139); Sassafras Nursery, Pamela Ingram (75 top and middle); Marilyn and Harrison Schafer; Mr. John Schuler (108–109); Michael Schultz, landscape design (86, 111 top and bottom); Michael Sedor, gardener; Mrs. R. R. Smith; Mrs. Thomas J. G. Spang; Judy and Michael Steinhardt (129, 130, 131, 136); Ann Swanson (142); Trudi and William Temple (84); Thompson & Morgan, for contributing seeds for experiments for this book; Mrs. Carol Valentine, landscape designed by Isabelle Greene; Mrs. Georgia Vance, Mazie Shank, and Cathy Coyle (7 middle, 38, 92 bottom right, 148–149, 150, 154, 155, 156, 157, 161, 162); Mr. and Mrs. Steve Vernon (74 top); Mr. and Mrs. André Viette, Viette Farm and Nursery (6 bottom, 82 right, 89 bottom, 90 bottom, left and right, 100 top, 115 bottom); Wave Hill, Marco Polo Stufano; Shelby White and Leon Levy; Bunny Williams (21 top, 123, 132 top, 133, 143); Mr. and Mrs. Richard P. Williams (36); Mr. and Mrs. James J. Wilson and their gardener Robbie Goldie (56–57, 72, 73); Woodrow Wilson Birthplace and Museum, Patricia Hobbs (161); Glenn Withey and Charles Price, landscape design (78–79, 80, 87, 95 top left, 95 bottom); Linda Yang (35, 135 top); Catherine Ziegler, landscape design; Robin Zitter, horticulturist.

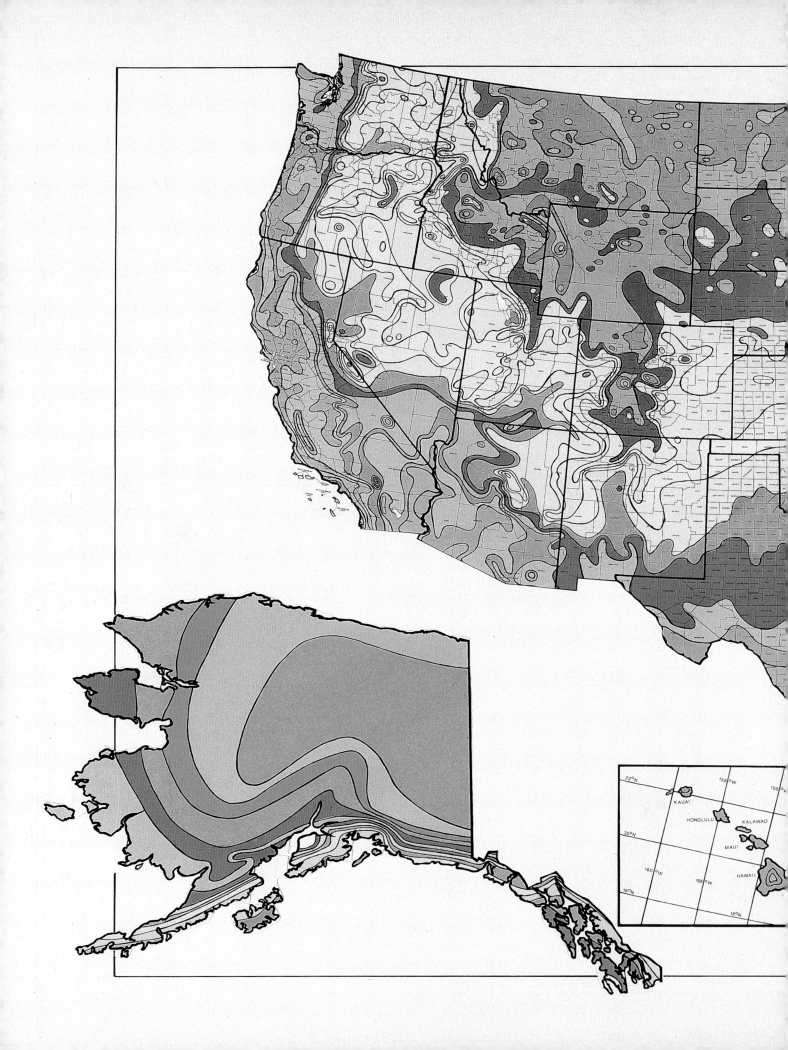

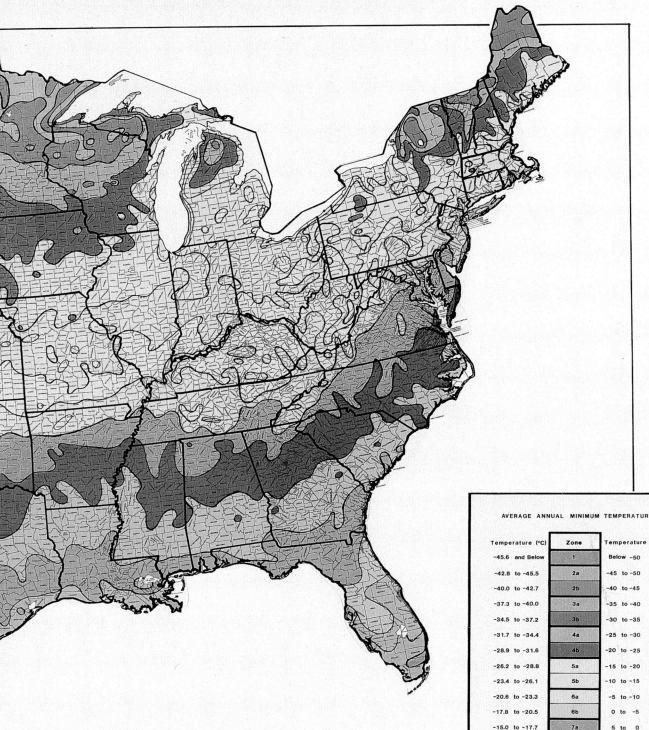

AVERAGE ANNUAL MINIMUM TEMPERATURE

Temperature (°C)	Zone	Temperature (°F)
-45.6 and Below	1	Below -50
-42.8 to -45.5	2a	-45 to -50
-40.0 to -42.7	2b	-40 to -45
-37.3 to -40.0	3a	-35 to -40
-34.5 to -37.2	3b	-30 to -35
-31.7 to -34.4	4a	-25 to -30
-28.9 to -31.6	4b	-20 to -25
-26.2 to -28.8	5a	-15 to -20
-23.4 to -26.1	5b	-10 to -15
-20.6 to -23.3	6a	-5 to -10
-17.8 to -20.5	6b	0 to -5
-15.0 to -17.7	7a	5 to 0
-12.3 to -15.0	7b	10 to 5
-9.5 to -12.2	8a	15 to 10
-6.7 to -9.4	8b	20 to 15
-3.9 to -6.6	9a	25 to 20
-1.2 to -3.8	9b	30 to 25
1.6 to -1.1	10a	35 to 30
4.4 to 1.7	10b	40 to 35
4.5 and Above	11	40 and Above

Zonal information indicates the minimum winter temperature a plant can withstand. However, humidity, rainfall, altitude, and maximum summer temperatures in your area are also critical factors to consider when buying plants and seeds. Sea breezes and salt may be important considerations in some cases. Southern gardeners may wish to consult *Herbaceous Perennial Plants,* by Allan M. Armitage, a general reference on perennials that contains authoritative findings on the summer hardiness of many plants. And keep in mind your property's own microclimates; often a plant that languishes in one part of the garden will perk up when moved to a different spot.

Designed by Amanda Wilson
Composed in Centaur
Produced by Mandarin Offset
Printed and bound in Hong Kong